THE ORGANIZATION

IN A CHANGING ENVIRONMENT

THE ORGANIZATION
IN A CHANGING ENVIRONMENT

RICHARD J. C. ROEBER
*Imperial College of Science
and Technology, London*

ADDISON-WESLEY PUBLISHING COMPANY
Reading, Massachusetts
Menlo Park, California · London · Don Mills, Ontario

This book is in the Addison-Wesley series:

ORGANIZATION DEVELOPMENT

Editors
Edgar Schein
Warren Bennis
Richard Beckhard

ISBN 0-201-06501-0
BCDEFGHIJK-CO-79876543

FOREWORD

Since the publication of the original series of six books on organization development (OD), this field has grown rapidly. No longer is it a field in search of a clear self-definition. We now find a large number of books and articles on OD and many competing models of what OD is and should be. All this proliferation of conceptualizing, empirical research, and description of new OD tools is a healthy and welcome development. Apparently, organizations have found that concepts and techniques of organization development are useful and viable, and schools have found that the theory and practice of planned change in organizations is a useful part of their curriculum.

One area of concern that received insufficient attention in the original series was the relationship of the organization to its *environment.* Only the Lawrence and Lorsch volume dealt explicitly with this problem, yet it continues to be one of the most fruitful areas for further exploration. The environment is changing rapidly, and the impact of this change on organizational structure and process must be clearly understood if OD efforts are to remain relevant to organizational realities. The present set of three books takes three quite different perspectives toward this problem in the hope of further stimulating thought and practice.

At the most general level, one can think of the environment as generating a set of values which influence organizational functioning and managerial thought. Roeber has written in a broad vein to describe what some of these value changes have been in the last several decades and how such changes have influenced managerial thinking. At a somewhat more specific level, the environment is a source of information for an organization, and the organization must learn how to process increasingly larger quantities and more complex categories of information. Galbraith addresses this problem by relating how different forms of organization structure have evolved in response to increasingly difficult problems of information processing. Although the analysis of organization structure has always been a difficult problem to deal with systematically, Galbraith has found a way to bring order to this complex area by building on previous theories and integrating them around his information-processing view of organizations.

The environment can also be thought of in more concrete physical terms. Work takes place in a physical environment and is influenced by the nature of that physical environment, yet virtually no attention is paid to the systematic analysis and manipulation of this portion of the environment. Steele gives us a clear view of some of the issues, provides a diagnostic scheme for the analysis of the environment, and suggests how organizations can set about to create physical environments which are more congruent with organizational goals.

As in our first series, we have not attempted to integrate the work of the different authors. Each gives us his view and his particular perspective on how to use that view to improve organizational functioning. We hope that the reader will be stimulated by these views to better understand his own organization and to begin some new organization development efforts.

March 1973

Edgar H. Schein
Richard Beckhard
Warren G. Bennis

PREFACE

Fifty years ago there would have been no point in writing this book. Ten years ago, while there would have been some point, the need would hardly have been recognized. But in the last ten years changes in our social environment have come upon us so abundantly and rapidly that there is no ignoring their effects inside the organization. The social environment has become turbulent and the old assumptions about decision-making – which limited managerial interest in the company's environment to commercially salient factors such as markets for products, raw materials, labor, technology, and the competition – no longer hold.

The pressures are felt within companies from the attitudes and expectations of an increasingly educated, demanding, and powerful workforce. They are felt from overt action by consumerist and environmentalist groups, calling companies to account for the social and ecological consequences of their commercial practice. They are imported with new entrants who do not share the assumptions of the existing managers.

Such pressures are more subtle in their effects than those from economic and technological change, for example, whose exponential growth rates are so often shaken in our faces by the doomwatchers. They are interrelated in complex ways and appear as problems – strikes, campus and other protests, low morale in the workforce, bitter rejection of business from outside, the breakdown of authority – to which the obvious short-term response is to seek solutions that ameliorate the effects of the problems. But a solution that deals with the problems in their presented forms cannot do more than "track" the far deeper, more fundamental changes under the surface of society, of which the problems are only a manifestation. It attacks symptoms rather than attempting to anticipate the future directions of change. And these changes are significant. They are profoundly affecting basic assumptions about what work people should do and about relationships at the workplace; they are forcing a redefinition of the role of commercial organizations in society.

The purpose of this book is to examine the nature and direction of the underlying changes and to make some guesses about their likely effects within organizations. The basic thesis is that the salient changes in the social environment are being generated by the release of constraints upon individual behavior. These constraints are exercised by the many systems — social systems, value systems, economic systems — that make up society and of which individuals are members, each standing at a place defined by his simultaneous membership in many overlapping systems. The constraints are being released by changes at many levels: technological changes, changed perceptions of the world through education and the influence of mass communications, and the decline of religion, among them. The leading change, in my opinion, is the increase in the wealth of Western industrialized society. This has relaxed the grip of the economic systems — which in turn consolidate the grip of many of the other systems — by giving individuals greater freedom of choice. This freedom can appear in very small but highly significant ways: one job implies slavery; the opportunity to choose between two jobs, even if neither is particularly attractive, is something closer to freedom, since it allows the individual the exercise of choice in his own interest. And it appears in the much more obvious ways apparent in the life style of the West Coast of the USA.

Indeed, the USA is probably the first society in history where the substantial majority of the inhabitants live in the secure expectation of material well-being. Many more admirable societies have existed — gentler, more humane, more intellectually or aesthetically aware, with a stronger sense of public service. But none where the choices that give society its shape and texture are so widely available. If the USA seems, in contrast to Europe, a "working-class" society, it is because the cultural norms are provided by the economically dominant majority. And if the USA seems wracked by problems that could destroy it, these are symptoms of this freedom.

It is this that makes the USA so exciting a country for a visitor, because it is where the future lies for good or ill. The USA is the leading edge of social change in the world. And if these changes do not result in total anarchy and self-destruction, they are leading to something like a "voluntary society" – a society in which the individual's membership in economic, cultural, and other systems is voluntary and not coerced. Seen this way, Women's Lib is a movement to assert the right of women to decide what being a woman shall mean for them. For workers it will mean the right of self-determination at their workplaces.

For the company, operating within an increasingly turbulent social environment, the instinctive response is defensive: to hold hard to the known; to deal with the symptoms while hoping that nothing more serious has changed. (And this is a necessary instinct. Resistance to change is a basic property of all systems and essential to their survival.) The real content of such changes will emerge with time. The disaffection of workers and a growing refusal to be subordinated to optimal engineering systems are more than irresponsibility or wrecking destructiveness. The system is losing its power to coerce workers into modes of behavior that are desirable to it. In response, the individual is asserting his own right of free choice. If he asserts this freedom in ways that are costly to the organization, it may be that he is not being given a more constructive alternative. Thus if companies wish to continue in business, they will have to learn ways of eliciting a voluntary commitment from their employees.

SOME ASSUMPTIONS ABOUT ORGANIZATIONS

The discussion in this book rests on the fundamental assumption that organizations are not closed systems, obedient to their own laws, but are open systems, sensitive and responsive to change in their environment. We can call them systems because they have boundaries (although these are not easy to define) and the capacity for self-perpetuation and growth. They are "open" because they exist by interchange of matter, energy, and information with the environment and its transformation within the boundaries.

The fundamental purpose of the organization, as of all systems, is its survival or the maintenance of its internal stability. But this subsumes a multiplicity of objectives and functions through which the stability is achieved, involving multiple interactions with the environment.

The organization itself consists of a number of dynamically interdependent subsystems, changes in any of which are likely to affect other subsystems. In the same way, the organization is itself a subsystem in an environment which consists of many more, all dynamically interdependent.

Such a definition immediately raises problems. If it is theoretically correct to describe organizations as open systems, they have presumably always been that. But in the past the effects within a system of changes in the social environment have not been the explicit concern of managers. Managers have quite successfully been able to make their decisions on the assumption that organizations are closed systems. The change that this shift reflects is in some senses the subject of the book. It is a change in the *rate* of social change and the effects of this on the salience of environmental factors in decision-making.

It is obvious enough that society changes constantly, the different systems within it at different rates. Over time the changes have been immense — something which I go into in more detail in Chapter 2. Within a shorter time span they have taken the form of many small adjustments, any of them within the capacity of the people in the organization to assimilate and adapt to "naturally." Thus organizations have been able to adapt themselves to slow changes in their social environment by making small concessions to pressures, and through the import of new personnel and the diffusion of new ideas. Through these unstructured, untutored, and unconscious adaptive responses organizations have "tracked" changes in their environment, much as the rear wheels of a long trailer track the changes in direction at the front. But such natural processes are no longer appropriate when the environment changes rapidly. Companies learned early in industrial history to deal consciously and explicitly with rapid fluctuations in their commercial environment; they will have to learn a more conscious response to changes in their social environment.

Techniques like Organization Development are designed precisely for this purpose: to focus attention on problems that have not traditionally been recognized as such and to devise methods for handling them. But managers will have to go still further and learn to scan their social environment for salient change. More than anything, they will need to acquire an awareness and understanding of the pressures for change, their direction and likely importance.

SCHEME OF THE BOOK

The plan of the book is straightforward, falling into three parts:

1. Starting from the basic assumption about the importance of environmental influences within the organization, the first five chapters examine the nature of social change, its force and direction, and its power for action within organizations. The conclusion is that the main direction of change is "toward a voluntary society," challenging many basic assumptions of management and possibly enforcing different patterns of working.

2. Chapters 6 and 7 examine two case studies of the response of organizations to changes in their environment. The first describes a British company which entered into a massive OD change program after shifts in the commercial environment revealed deficiencies in union and management practices. The second deals with the response of oil companies in the Middle East to a changing political environment.

3. The last seven chapters discuss in more detail the effects of social change within the organization. Two areas are examined: pressures for change originating outside the organization, leading to a redefinition of its role in society; and pressures originating inside, leading to changes in workplace relationships and the nature of jobs.

I have set the discussion in the context of economic changes that are widely relevant. It is focused primarily on the USA, because the social changes which are its main subject are being first encountered there. It hardly needs to be said that the differences between the USA and Europe are such as to make any direct comparison misleading. Nonetheless I am certain that the problems emerging for organizations as a result of this greater freedom of personal choice will emerge elsewhere in some form as the level of ambient wealth rises. The signs are there in industrial disaffection and in student unrest; the more profound changes – or something like them – will follow as European economic development follows that of the USA.

References have been kept to a minimum, largely because not much is written in this particular area, and an uncontrollable volume of partly relevant literature would simply overwhelm the reader. I have made a number of references in the text to such writers as Maslow, MacGregor, and Herzberg without further explanation, since their work is so well-known that, if the reader has managed to escape learning about them, he will have no difficulty in tracking down references.

London, England
March 1973

R.J.C.R.

CONTENTS

Summary 133

13 Internal Pressures: Anticipating Change 135

    Role of management 139
    Summary 142

14 Democratic Organizations 143

    Overview 153
    Organizations: structure and behavior 153
    Changes in the social environment 154
    Pressures on the corporation 156

1
HIDDEN FUTURES

If we knew where to look, we would find the future in our midst. The elements that will shape our lives in the next generation are already with us; the hardware and software of the future, the systems of values, technologies, and business — all are among us in different stages of ripeness. Most of them are familiar and fully explored. It is from our understanding of these known systems whose basic properties seem unlikely to change that we extrapolate for our understanding of the future. Other systems lie around us in embryo, as do the future popes, presidents, painters, and revolutionary leaders who are already scattered around the world, secretly preparing themselves in cradles. Like those babies, these emergent systems reveal too little of themselves to catch our attention, and what little they do reveal comes in ways too ambiguous to understand. Even if we catch a fleeting glimpse, we almost certainly misinterpret what we see. Our eyes are trained by experience; and the past, for this purpose, is always out of date.

It is for this reason that changes which are continuous present themselves to us as discontinuities — more particularly so as the rate of change increases. The process of change is continuous, like changes in the landscape resulting from a lengthy process of wearing and fretting by wind and rain. But our perceptions of reality, the models against which we measure the observed world, change discontinuously, like the earthquakes which redistribute the stresses built up at the surface of the earth.

There was a time — not long ago — when the models of behavior, assumptions, and proper relationships which a man acquired while growing up would last him through his life without strain. But that time is in the past, and the half-life of these "life models" may be down to a decade or so. Like the engineer whose skills are obsolete five years after he acquires them, we may have to face a life of continual re-education, if as individuals we are to be usefully engaged in our environment. The problem faces organizations no less than individuals, although here it is not so much a matter of changing mental models as of changing structures, the physical embodiment of the internal model. And for an organization to do this requires a more conscious and explicit view of the future.

All companies periodically ask themselves the question, "Where are we going?" And the answer will be based on concrete information about products, financing, markets, growth targets, competition, technology, and anything else that seems relevant. If this is part of a planning exercise, it will lead to decisions about capital investment, research, and acquisitions. It may also contain information about the numbers of people and skills needed at certain points along the way, perhaps (but rarely) pointing to some such positive decision as funding a program of research and teaching. Or it may raise questions about organization such as, for example, about the control structure appropriate to a rapidly expanding overseas operation. Logically speaking, such human factors are secondary considerations, merely the byproducts of the primary decisions about investment, profit targets, and the rest. It would not make much sense to plan to acquire a pool of particular skills without any idea of how they are to be used.

But this order of priority is only possible on the basis of a fairly large assumption: that the human environment around the organization is, for the purposes of planning, constant; that it laps around the foundations of the organization like an endless sea so that no planning more sophisticated than the decision to buy a bucket is needed to ensure an adequate supply. Companies do plan for their human needs, but even the most elaborate manpower plan assumes a high degree of constancy in the human material. This situation is changing — not in the sense that people are growing three legs, but in the more insidious sense that they are not the same people. The needs and demands of individual workers are changing, and the requirements of society are changing. And as the rate of change increases, the effects are being felt (although hardly yet recognized for what they are) inside organizations whose managers have hitherto been able to ignore such factors. Companies will have to learn to pay close attention to the directions of social change and to anticipate its effects, if they are not going to be overwhelmed by it as surely as companies have been overwhelmed by the more expected changes in their markets or technology in the past.

It is not that society has been constant in the past: almost the only constant factor in society *is* change. But the rate of change has been such that organizations have been able to adapt to its consequences in ways that are "natural" – that is, unstructured, unconscious, and evolutionary in their effects. Thus the management makes concessions to the pressures within the organization, of which the most obviously effective are those exerted by unions for changed working conditions, shorter working hours, and more money; new ideas filter in with changes in technology which may enforce changes in the methods of work – as, for example, with a change from batch to continuous-process working or with increases in scale and complexity of a process and the concomitant increase in the workers' responsibility; renewal of the organization's membership brings in change from the environment, however powerful the socializing effect of working through to positions of influence. Because the resulting adjustments within the organization are small, they can be accommodated by the existing social structure of the company without seeming to threaten it. But the cumulative effect over time is large. We have only to think back twenty years to ruling assumptions about the "rights" of managers and the whole question of authority within a hierarchical organization; to hiring practices and treatment of unions; to corporate sensitivity to external pressures over issues like pollution or despoliation of natural amenities; to the attitudes, manners, and dress that were thought to be appropriate to a young man with ambitions. The extent of these "natural" changes is examined in more detail in the next chapter. Let it suffice at this stage to comment that over time they have amounted to an accumulation of change which a few decades back would have been regarded as revolutionary.

But the rate of change has now increased beyond the capacity of natural adaptive processes. The environment has become turbulent and the directions of change apparently random; they force themselves upon a manager as part of the complex array of data he must consider in planning for the future. Some more conscious process of adaptation is needed.

Perhaps the clearest simple example of the effects of social change on business decisions is the influence of turbulence from the environmentalist antipollution lobby on the investment decisions of erstwhile polluters. However toughly cynical the managers of paper companies might be when considering a new pulp mill in a remote part of Oregon, they must now build into their decision some calculations concerning possible actions by the state and federal governments or by pressure groups and weigh them against the costs of investing in pollution control.

A less clear-cut example is given by the experience of a major European dyestuffs company now facing a complete upheaval in its operations, arguably because it did not make a series of smaller, planned changes in the past 15 years. The company has been successfully in business for nearly a century, during which time its business has become increasingly international and competitive. The main constraints on success arose from the marketing side (leading to intense competition with prices and technical services) and technological innovation. The managers prided themselves in being technically first-class and managerially tough — and in no area more so than that of production. In engineering terms the processes are simple: in each reaction stage batches of chemicals are stirred under given conditions, crystallized, and filtered. Cumulatively they are complex, since some dyes involve 40 reaction stages. The process is labor-intensive and few skills are needed. Because of the unpleasant nature of the work, the company's plants have tended to become the employer of last resort where other employers existed.

From time to time the management considered investing in mechanical filters or in some continuous process plant. But the cost never justified the investment, even though some of the plants were as old as the company. With the small batches involved, a more elaborate plant was too expensive; there was no lack of the necessary unskilled labor to operate the messy old plants, and more could be procured from less-developed parts of Europe and Asia Minor if the need arose. This decision not to invest was reinforced by the insistence of the salespeople that the company should provide a "full range" of dyes — many of them of extreme complexity and low sales volume — to meet their competition. But it made the company doubly vulnerable: to higher wages and to a shortage of workers. The company is now facing the prospect of eliminating up to three-quarters of its dyes and has mounted a crash program of investment in a single mechanized plant. But it may be too late. The competition has preempted the most attractive part of the bulk market, leaving the vulnerable high-cost low-volume products alone. It may be that the company will have to cease operations altogether within the next five years.

The point in this case is that the company failed to anticipate changes in its human environment — specifically, conditions in which workers would do unpleasant work only at uneconomically high wages. It is easy to see this in retrospect, but it was extremely difficult to have seen it from within the culture of the company at the time. Nonetheless, it would have been possible to predict the effects of such broad and sustained trends in the labor market, if a systematic effort had been made; the evidence was all there. The result has been a crisis and an apparent discontinuity. The changes that brought it about were continuous.

EMERGENT SYSTEMS

If companies are to scan their environment for significant change, they will have to devise techniques for spying out systems that have the power to affect our lives in the future. A gardener weeding his flower beds in Spring knows what his favorite plants look like when their leaves are just showing, and he does not pull them out with the weeds. But if every season brought a random crop of completely new plants, he would be hard-pressed to garden at all. Scanning our social environment, we find that we are in the latter situation. We see many signs of change but cannot easily assess their true significance. Parents cannot know whether their drug-taking, sexually promiscuous, politically active, dropping-out children are the bright-faced harbingers of a new golden age — as the romantic myth tells us — or merely delinquent. They are likely to assume the latter view, if only because their own mental models of child behavior were formed in different times. Older managers fall into the same trap when they assume that workers ought to be punctual, hard-working, obedient, and respectful toward authority, and that they are somehow morally at fault if they fail to meet these standards. To people with a religious upbringing, the frightening rate at which the eternal truths of society are being dropped is a sure sign of moral failure and directly attributable to the decline in church-going. These interpretations may be correct or they may be erroneous. What they certainly are is an attempt to judge new events against existing standards.

New systems of thought are usually misread when they first appear, because they are in opposition to the old systems and stand judged by them. Also, they make their first appearance in misleading ways, often assuming the clothing of that which they will replace. The delinquent child is still a child, and rioting workers do productive work when they are not rioting. This is a variant of the frequently noted fact that technological

change always assumes the clothing of what it is replacing. Early Chinese porcelain was made in the shape of bronze vessels; the motor car first appeared as a carriage, even with whip pockets (in Britain car-body makers are still called "coach makers"). Rayon first appeared as "artificial silk" and plastic as imitation leather, wood, or whatever. The new systems — emergent systems, as Dr. Fred Emery calls them — are weak, and the signals they give out are feeble.* A corollary of this disguised growth is that once they have emerged they are too strong and vigorous to destroy. The picketing by coal miners of electricity power stations during the 1972 coal strike in Britain was just such a case. As a manifestation of the breakdown of some commonly agreed-upon restraints, it was too strong to be opposed except by the use of force which the country would not have tolerated.
in recent years:

   Urban breakdown, race riots, Black Power

   Consumerism, product safety, cigarette health warning, *Unsafe at Any Speed*

   Industrial unrest, strikes, Charles Chaplin's *Modern Times*

   Malicious damage in factories, absenteeism, high turnover

   Unisex, long hair, communes, sexual promiscuity

   Breakup of the family, *Rebel Without a Cause*, delinquency

   Environmentalism, conservationism, antipollution, *The Silent Spring*

   Radical and revolutionary politics, antiwar, anti-Pentagon, office bombing

   Antiindustry sentiment, dropping out, the beat generation

   Drug culture, pop culture, rock-and-roll hysteria

   Student violence, "trashing," student-worker alliance

   Women's Lib, Gay Lib, "radical chic"

   Hippies, flower power, Eastern-style mysticism, Zen

   Each of these diverse movements (or events or ideas) made its first appearance in the midst of many others, and the nature of that first

---

*Emery, F.E., and E.L. Trist, *Towards a Social Ecology*. London: Plenum Publications, 1972.

appearance gave little clue to its ultimate development. For every lucky social commentator who instantly divined the true underlying importance of, say, *Rebel Without a Cause*, there were thousands who muttered darkly about delinquency and "the breakdown of society as we know it." Similarly, there were many trend spotters who jumped swiftly onto the passing bandwagon of the hippie movement, for example, or the beat generation, or pop art, only to find it running out of gas a few yards down the road. Other movements which have considerable importance began quietly and even suffered false deaths: the progress of environmentalism since the publication of Rachel Carson's *The Silent Spring* has been thus misleading.

The signals given out by new systems are weak and easily confused by "noise" from others. (I call them "systems," although they are actually cultural, economic, social, or ideological phenomena, because they have boundaries — admittedly fuzzy — and because they grow and die like other systems.) As they start to break through the surface of our perceptions, a wide range of interpretations are consistent with the signals they give out. Because choice is not enforced by scientific logic, the interpretation that an individual favors will tend to have less to do with any objective assessment of the observed data than with his more subjective preferences. As in the development of a scientific hypothesis, new facts are stretched over the skeleton of the old theory. As more information accumulates, the effort becomes greater until the less vital system gives way; either the old is junked or the new is killed. In this exercise of fitting, nothing is more eagerly grasped than the familiar, the data that fits the favored preconception.

When Miss Carson's book, *The Silent Spring*, first appeared, her thesis — that the complex chemicals used in agricultural pest control were potentially devastating to wild life — gathered fervent supporters. The budding environmentalist movement that this represented could, however, be comfortably fitted into the "little old ladies in tennis shoes" or "hysterical nut-eaters" categories by anyone (which at the time included me) who found the new information too disturbing to accept or who, like the pesticide manufacturers, were directly threatened by it. On the other hand, the supporters of Miss Carson had their own preconceptions, specifically a gloomy but half-relishing willingness to believe that "they" were poisoning us all. Neither set of preconceptions led to distinguished evaluations of the underlying issues. It was left to more methodical studies to generate the data which led to the ban on chlorinated hydrocarbons and probably, before long, on much else besides.

The only clue we have to the future development of these emergent systems, given the confusing nature of the signals they emit, lies in some judgment about their latent underlying energy. A race riot must be seen, and in the short run dealt with, as a piece of destructive lawlessness. But the strength of a movement like Black Power rests not in the surface phenomena of rioting but in the injustices of racial discrimination. If Black Power became a proscribed organization and its leaders jailed, the issue would still be full of energy. Similarly, if General Motors had succeeded in so discrediting Ralph Nader that he disappeared from public view, they would at best have only delayed an inevitable public reaction against the big-corporation usurpation of consumer's right of choice. The consumer movement would have continued to grow whether or not it was spearheaded in its active phase by an attack on the motor car; the energy of the underlying system would not have been touched.

Therefore I have listed the latent energy of the underlying issues in a descending order as I see it. Readers will doubtless disagree with ranking and are free to provide their own; what is important is the reasoning behind it.

Among the lower energy systems I have placed the hippie movement, Women's Lib, dropping-out, and revolutionary politics. Among the higher energy systems are industrial unrest, Black Power, consumerism, "unisex," and environmentalism. Thus the hippie movement was short-lived because it did not provide an answer to the social problems against which it reacted, and dropping-out is but a weak response to real problems. Although very visible and often fashionable, the violent forms of social change proposed by revolutionary groups would be disproportionately destructive ways of dealing with the problems of Western countries; I cannot believe they will succeed because I don't think the conditions are right. There is not enough latent energy in the underlying issues or, to put it another way, not enough injustice in the system. (In Chapter 5, however, we will see that there might be, if certain conditions arise from present directions of social change.) Women's Lib and the "unisex" trend are the exact mirror images of each other. Women's Lib is a highly specific and structured system which overtly attacks "sexism" only to create a new discrimination. Fundamentally, it has its roots in a diffuse and energyless area of individual rather than social problems. The tendency of young men and women to dress and appear more alike is, by contrast, a highly significant but diffuse reaction against the ethic of sexual exploitation (or, at best, of sexual warfare) exemplified by the "Hemingway man" and his direct descendant, Playboy culture.

At the other end of the scale, Black Power is vital, and (spared the internal troubles that always overtake extremist political movements) it has the strength for growth because of the energy latent in the tensions of racial injustice. Consumerism has its roots in the manifest inability of market forces to provide society with many of the nonmarket goods it needs. Industrial unrest will continue to become more threatening to the industrial order until the tension between human nature and the inhuman demands of optimally designed engineering systems is resolved — probably in the interests of the human. The whole environmentalism-antipollution-conservationism cluster has very mixed origins. But the issues will have energy, and the system will have strength for growth, while the present abuses continue.

SOME SCENARIOS FOR THE FUTURE

These changes will combine to form our future. Many alternative futures have been proposed. Herman Kahn of the Hudson Institute has suggested in the book, *The Year 2000,* that we are headed toward a "post-industrial" society of which some characteristics are the increasing importance of service industries, high per-capita income with effective floor on income and welfare, a diminishing role of the market compared to public sector, and an erosion among the middle classes of work-oriented values. These would be social characteristics of a society in which production and selling — predominant in the existing consumer-oriented society — yielded to service activities.

But before we arrived at this stage we would experience a period characterized by discontinuous change, according to Peter Drucker's book, *The Age of Discontinuity.* The leading characteristics of this change might be the growth and eventual domination of industry by "knowledge" industries, the increasing internationalization of markets and industries to the point of the emergence of a world economy, and the domination of our lives by large governmental and industrial groups, with a corresponding threat to the individual. In *The New Industrial State* John Kenneth Galbraith is more specific. He discusses the continuing growth and domination of markets by producers who use the tools of mass persuasion to reduce risk and uncertainty in their own environments and the closer integration of government and industry (hence the title of the book) into a single coordinated unit. Alvin Toffler describes the effect that these changes produce on individuals in *Future Shock*, an effect which he defines as ". . . the shattering stress and disorientation we induce in individuals by subjecting them to too much change in too short a time. . ." The changes Toffler writes about derive mainly from continuing technological advances, particularly in the areas of communications and transportation. He describes the accelerating rate of change in terms that are extended and carried forward in Kahn's list of "100 technical innovations very likely in the last third of the twentieth century." However, these advances carry a cost; the ecologists, environmentalists, conservationists, and doomwatchers forecast the limits that are set, sometimes drastically, by pollution and the finiteness of global resources. A leading example is Jay Forrester of MIT, commissioned by the Club of Rome to construct a "world dynamics model" as a tool to investigate these effects. According to this model, the world could be facing a holocaust in 50 to 100 years if the developed world does not immediately adopt nongrowth economic and population policies.

We have presented side-by-side a variety of forecasts. Give or take an assumption or two, they are not inconsistent with one another. And they suggest some patterns which may help us to focus on the problem of forecasting social change:

1. Integrative/Disintegrative Changes. The dominant mode of change that has characterized the economic development of the industrialized West is integrative — the knitting-together of systems into closer dependencies and larger units. Integrative change is the product of the pursuit of efficiency and/or profit; the mode of operation is the elimination of slack within and between systems. It is assumed to be the mode of change in most of the predictions. Kahn, however, goes a stage further and speculates on the sort of industry that will emerge — if it emerges at all — on the other side. His "post-industrial" society is characterized by what one may call disintegrative change, individual will and appetites becoming more important.

2. Extrapolative/Nonextrapolative Forecasting. Most prediction, however intuitive, is based on the extrapolation forward of the observed behavior of systems whose characteristics are assumed either to remain constant or to change in predictable ways over the relevant period. Thus these predictions have clear origins in present society: service industries grow; companies become larger; Japan mushrooms; governments take even closer interest in industries; per-capita consumption continues to increase; people become yet more dwarfed and dominated by the huge systems that information technology makes possible. Yet many of the systems that are going to be important in our futures are not yet recognized for their potential. Delphi methods of forecasting are an attempt to generate nonextrapolative pointers to the future. Forrester's dynamic modeling techniques provide a more systematic approach to this problem since the models can generate behavior that would not have been predicted from the starting assumptions.

The social changes that concern us in this book are almost entirely disintegrative in their effects on society. That is, they are the results of an enlargement of the individual's area of self-determination. While the most important changes are visible and forecastable — as were the changes in the European dyestuffs company described earlier — many of them cannot be forecast. Either they are invisible, puzzling presences, the true strength of which we cannot gauge, or they are the logical results of other changes.

However, the dominant systems in society do not change so rapidly or dramatically as the emergent systems we have discussed in this chapter. On the contrary, our world is still dominated by systems of which the behavior is relatively constant or which, if it changes, does so in fairly predictable ways. The peculiar problem of today is one of adjustment to the specific areas of change that are both rapid and unpredictable. But before considering this problem I shall attempt to put it in the perspective of the changes that have taken place over past decades. The 1970's must have seemed unimaginably distant to anyone peering into the murk of the future from the beginning of the century, and the changes that have taken place in the seven decades since then are, almost literally, unimaginable.

SUMMARY

Because the human environment of industry once changed slowly and in relatively predictable ways, it was possible in the past to make business decisions on the implicit assumption that this environment was constant — that is, on the assumption that the human organization was a closed system. But the environment is now changing more rapidly and in unpredictable ways. Its influence is being felt inside the boundaries of the organization, and social change is becoming a factor in business decisions.

Companies must take an organized view of the directions of social change. But, while this may be effective in predicting broad trends, it is more difficult to assess accurately the power with which new social and value systems will affect us in the future. The emergent systems are trebly disguised: by the confusion of noise that overwhelms their signals when they are weak; by their habit of "parasitic" growth from within themselves; and by our inability to look at them with new eyes. A more objective judgment can only come from an understanding of the energy latent in tensions underlying these emergent systems.

Many different futures have been projected. Although seemingly headed in different directions, they contain common elements. Most significantly, they point to a tension between the forces of "integrative" change — continuing the processes of economic and technological change of the past century — and the increasingly powerful forces of "disintegrative" change — resulting from the freer exercise of individual choice.

2
CONTINUOUS REVOLUTIONS

Viewed separately and at a moment in time, the processes of change are slow and seemingly without purposeful effect. Hence we have the appeal of direct action. But in sum, and over time, such slow processes amount to a revolution — thinly spread. Demands for "revolution now" only serve to underline just how much has been achieved without it. Any consideration of the effects of future social change on the organization should therefore be set in the context of changes whose continuity extends back to and beyond the turn of the century. Since then, the organization has undergone changes that would have been labeled Bolshevik in the previous generation and are still so regarded by some people.

It is the assumption of this book that social change is the manifestation of shifts in the underlying power structure of society. We shall therefore start this discussion with a very schematic survey of the main directions of change in the relationships among government, business, and the individual — who is both worker and consumer.

Table 1 indicates some of the main areas of change, expressed as the transfer of power between sectors. Before we proceed to a more detailed discussion, two points should be made:

- The net shifts of power over the last half-century have been enormously to the benefit of government. By comparison, industry

Table 1. Some elements of power

Accruing to:	Government	Industry	Individual
In relation to:			
Government		Increased spending on defense and research Closer integration: more influence within government Common interests Power to influence economic management, regional planning, etc.	Welfare benefits Education Growing sensitivity to popular pressure in government
Industry	Economic management macro (fiscal, monetary) micro (detailed intervention) regional Resource management pollution planning controls Social interventions antitrust workers' conditions, right to work, etc.		Legislated protection Choice of jobs and location Choice in spending higher pay; increased discretionary income Countervailing power of unions
Individual	Effects of economic policies taxation demand management income policies Unresponsive machinery of government; more pervasive powers Management of public opinion	Size Power over jobs Technology production admass manipulations organizational design; personal engineering	

has lost many degrees of freedom, and the individual has lost his capacity to influence events within the huge and increasingly complex government machine. As much as anything, this is a function of the far wider range of activities that are now found within government.

● None of the shifts is one-way. Thus the growth of public-sector spending has given the government great power and influence within industry. It has also given the industry power within government by extending the areas of contact and integrating activities in the two sectors. The individual has lost the power to affect many decisions that touch his life, but he is the beneficiary of many of the activities which these decisions represent, as in the case of welfare services.

There are six possible pairs which may be formed from the trio of government, industry, and the individual. What follows is a catalog of ways in which the first-named member of a pair has acquired elements of power from the second. Many of these shifts are small, but in sum they add up to massive shifts in the balance of power within society, and corresponding changes in assumptions about their relationships.

1. GOVERNMENT/COMPANIES

a) Management of the economy at a general level. Development of more sophisticated tools (fiscal and monetary) for maintaining a balance between growth, inflation, and the maintenance of full employment. Emergence of more tightly integrated international economic system which, through international currency control and a sensibility to balance of payments considerations, feeds back into the domestic economy.

b) Management of the economy at a detailed level.

   i)   Intervention in industry for economic ends; in the USA through the formation of regulatory agencies, in Europe through nationalization and "indicative planning."

   ii) Closer *de facto* involvement where the indivisibilities of investment in technological research and development draw the government in as the dominating source of funds and of influence, and where private industry is induced to play a part in such socially oriented policies as housing, urban renewal, black capitalism.

c)   Legislative restrictions on companies for social ends.

i)   Antitrust legislation, starting with the Sherman Act and evolving to the present day. (Although overtly economic in intent — preserving competition — the legislation had its origins in populist feeling against large units of power.)

ii)   The body of legislation which regulates and secures minimum standards of working conditions and safety for the worker, starting with the Factory Acts in Britain of more than a century ago.

iii)   Power over resource utilization. Planning restrictions on the use of land are an accepted part of life in Europe, where land is scarce (particularly in countries like Britain, Holland, and Denmark). Control of pollution has been a government concern in Britain for more than a century for the same reason. As resource "slack" is used up in the USA, similar planning powers can be expected to develop.

2.   GOVERNMENT/INDIVIDUAL

a)   Restrictions on the freedom to use or dispose of property at will through planning (mainly in Europe), and taxes on personal wealth — income and inheritance taxes — are general; wealth (i.e., capital) taxes are a feature of "socialistic" countries like Sweden.

b)   The development of welfare agencies, although in the interests of the individual, has given governments considerable influence in determining detailed aspects of individual lives. Again, this is a mainly European development. As the obverse of a development designed to secure benefits for the individual, it will be dealt with in Section 5, below.

c)   Declining effectiveness of existing institutions as expression of public will. This is a function of:

i)   Scale and complexity of government departments, which take on many more numerous and more complex jobs as the balance of spending power is swung (through the medium of taxes) into the public sector.

ii)   Emergence of "cabinet government," where the executive — which in the USA is not elected but appointed by the President, and in Europe consists of an inner cadre of elected and permanent officials — has acquired more power and is becoming increasingly isolated from the legislature. This is most apparent in Britain and throughout Europe; the device of Congressional and Senate committees gives US legislators a measure of real power.

iii) Rigidities of the party-political system as parties form on institutional lines. There emerges a party "machine" whose aim becomes more that of survival than of the political purpose from which it originated.

3. COMPANY/GOVERNMENT

a) Higher degree of integration through regulation and growing government purchasing power reduces relevant uncertainty in company environment. This was first apparent with the regulated utilities; it is now apparent in "client" industries such as aerospace and defense.

b) Consolidation of special interest groups with power enough to keep profitable anomalies (such as depletion allowances for petroleum companies) in existence. This is a form of market manipulation.

c) The move to multinational operation, which gives the companies considerable flexibility for minimizing tax liabilities.

4. COMPANY/INDIVIDUAL

a) Improvements in technique. Constant effort toward finding better ways of doing things has resulted in systems of production and organization to which the individual is subordinated for optimal functioning. These elements of improved design all represent improvements in efficiency or loss of slack within which the individual had some room to exercise his individuality.

b) The yen for size. Represents security for the corporation but results in units to which the individual cannot relate and for which he feels no commitment.

c) Market manipulation. The concurrent development of mass media and of techniques for mass persuasion (each supporting the other) has given the company the power to generate a demand for its products, resulting in a loss of sovereignty for the consumer.

d)   Use of resources. The unrestricted utilization of resources for profit has resulted in ugly cities, dead lakes, and smog. These represent costs which the businesses responsible did not have to bear but which, as population and standards of living have risen, are now impinging on the mass of people. The result is a gain to the company at the cost of the individual.

5.   INDIVIDUAL/GOVERNMENT

a)   Increased concern with welfare through pension schemes, medical care, unemployment benefits and state-supported housing projects (further developed in Europe than in the US). In effect, provision of a wider range of nonmarketable goods — such as security and health — which the private sector is not geared to provide.

b)   Education. This is now one of the major industries, providing more possibilities and more choice for the individual.

6.   INDIVIDUAL/COMPANY

a)   Growth of unions has given the individual countervailing power against employers. Together with the generally high levels of employment and high wages, this development has provided the individual with such powers as (b) and (c) below.

b)   Choice of job, a factor which has far-reaching implications for management.

c)   Improved material standards. The standard of living in the USA, measured solely in terms of consumption, is so far ahead of that in other parts of the world that the poor have ceased to be a class; they have become a problem. People are less easily exploited and coerced.

d)   Growth of consumerism promises to give the consumer countervailing power against the market power of the companies, a balance similar to that offered to labor by the development of unions.

This schematic discussion of shifts in power patterns obviously leaves out much that is of great importance. For example:

- The unions, like political parties, have been progressively pursuing other objectives than the best interests of their members, both in the USA and in Europe.

- The individual, although to some extent freed from the direct exercise of coercion by his employer through his own increased power in the labor market, is nonetheless enslaved by the patterns of demand which the system generates.

- Pressures are brought to bear on all the parties and institutions by a background of increasing population and an uncontrolled drift to unplanned cities.

The changed view of property is one of the most crucial shifts of the period. The industrial revolution created a class of property which carried no social obligations; the right of the owner to dispose of it as he chose was regarded as sacred and inalienable. But the last century has seen progressive encroachments on this right through income tax, inheritance tax, and (in land-hungry Europe) the assumption of planning powers over the use of land. The right to the enjoyment of property can now be said to be contingent on social will; it is a privileged and not an absolute access to resources which society may withhold. The contingent nature of this privilege is truer of the situation in Europe than in the USA. Indeed, not many Americans would accept the above definition of property as an accurate view of the US situation. But the slow accretion of laws which one way or another limit the rights of ownership point inevitably to that conclusion.

There are three essential points to make about these changes. First we must observe that, contrary to radical dogma, society is not static and in need of a revolution to get it moving again; society is fundamentally dynamic. Moreover, it is on the move in directions that give some reason for hope. The changes described in this chapter took place slowly, but over time they represent enormous shifts in society; not all of them are beneficial, but the tendency is one of correcting rather than adding to wrongs. If in the course of economic development new wrongs have appeared, we are in the middle of events — specifically the growth of the consumer movement — which will seek to redress them.

Second, it has not been a purposive planned process but a fumbling effort, including many false starts, lost hopes (as in the early development of the antitrust legislation), and missed opportunities. It is, in short, an evolutionary process through which society is constantly adapting to new conditions and thus creating new forces which in turn will generate still newer conditions. The problems we are wracked by today have been spawned by our attempts to deal with the problems of a century ago. The industrialized West has so successfully dealt with the problem of how to create wealth and, by some definitions, a good life for its people that it is now facing precisely the opposite problem: how to bring the wealth-creating part of society under some sort of control. And it is facing it because the increase in general wealth is loosening established relationships and creating the conditions in which people are free to question old assumptions.

Finally, the process has been gradual and organic so that its effects have been naturally assimilated. The distance traveled has been great, but it has been a journey taken in easy stages. It has been more effective than any revolution, because the changes have grown into society rather than been imposed upon it. It has also been less destructive than a revolution, which devours far more than just its children.

As society has changed, so have the organizations which exist within it — slowly, organically, naturally, without conscious design, by a process of trial and error. And the sum of change has been as great as that of the social environment. A manager who jumped forward from the turn of the century to today would find so much that was different he would probably find it impossible to manage. Even if it was possible to allow for changes in technology and the consequent changes in organization design, he would find a shift in the balance of power between the managers and the managed which amounted to a substantial devolution of decision-making power. (The shift has been tracked in the changing organization theories which, from Weber to Open Systems theorists, have been reflecting the change in contemporary preoccupations quite as much as they have been probing more deeply into organizations.) The move from owner-entrepreneur to shareholders and professional management; the move from a largely powerless working class to unionized workers and now, further, to workers with real power in a full employment economy; the segmentation and specialization of work in assembly-line operations; the more recent requirement for ever-more-sophisticated skills; the growth of education and the effects of it on workers' aspirations and, perhaps more powerfully, the effects of television and other mass media — these have brought about great changes within the organization, felt by management mostly as limitations on their freedom of action.

This period of organic adaptation is now ending. Society has changed greatly in the past few generations, but the rate of change has increased to a point where unconscious processes of change within an organization cannot handle the demands of a turbulent environment. We have entered a period in which there is required a more conscious redesign of organizations to *anticipate* the effects of change.

SUMMARY

Looking back to the turn of the century and beyond, it is apparent that society has been through not one but several revolutions. They have been thinly spread over time, taking the form of many small adjustments to changing conditions. The net result has been large changes in the balance of power among the systems that make up society, specifically among the individual, government, and private industry. These lead to the conclusion that society is fundamentally dynamic, changing through a process of evolutionary adaptation and at a rate that allows its parts to assimilate this change organically. When change in society is more rapid, more conscious processes of adaptation may be needed by organizations.

3
THE ROOTS OF CHANGE

To answer the question "Where is society headed?" we must go more deeply into the basic question of "Why is it moving?" Social change is a manifestation of shifts in the balance among the complexly linked systems of values, economies, and people that make up society. Even if the question of why the balance between these systems changes cannot be simply answered (the interactions are too complex), it may be possible to gain some understanding of the way in which they interact and the forces that they generate.

Many candidates are nominated by social commentators at any point in time for the role of the chief agent of change. Some current favorites are:

1. The issues around which change and protest center. According to this view – the here-and-now view of change – it is the injustices of modern society that have called into being the movements that aim to redress them. If we want to know why society is changing, we need look no further than at what needs to be changed: racial discrimination, corruption in public life, the inequitable distribution of wealth, urban squalor, the Vietnam War, exploitation of the Third World, and so on.

2. Generally available education – particularly college education, which has broadened the intellectual horizons of the young and provided a period of freedom in which to question the assumptions of their parents' world.

3. Technological change, particularly the vast increase in the speed and efficiency of communications and transport. This has altered our perceptions of the world, and so altered the world itself.

4. The growth of large organizations — the commercial organizations we work in, the cities we live in, and the government organizations that increasingly rule our lives. This growth has resulted in a loss of real community and individual indentity, and a growing powerlessness of the individual to influence the decisions that shape his life.

5. Specialization of work, which has made labor meaningless, robbed work of its joy, and turned men into machines to be fitted into other machines.

6. The pressure of population, which has reduced the space around people and generated a system of rules and restrictions without which large social organizations could not survive. The simplest model of restriction is the traffic light, which regulates our passage across intersections and is made necessary by high traffic density. At a more complex level, we cannot grant other people in cities the full humanity that we would in small communities.

7. Loss of a moral sense, which most precisely means loss of religious faith but also includes those value systems and the patterns of duties, rights, and obligations that Jean Jacques Rousseau called the "social contract."

8. Breakdown of the family, with its concomitant loss of respect for authority and for age.

Others have been suggested, but this limited list probably covers the main categories. How far can we nominate them as generators or originators of change?

1. Issues are by far the most seductive category. The flux of emotions that surround an issue in its own time is so strong as to dominate any sense of perspective. We feel so strongly about our issues — the Vietnam War, for example, or the growing power of Federal Government — that we ascribe to them a unique importance. The corollary follows that if something is not done, society will — or ought to — crash about our ears. But for this to

be true, either the issues have to be new or the people reacting to them so powerfully have to be, in some senses, new people.

The second argument is self-evidently untrue. It is nice to think, as embattled college presidents are fond of saying, that today's young people are more sensitive and intelligent than at any time in Man's history. They may be different in many ways, but in their basic equipment, genetically acquired, they comprise a population with the same amount of intelligence and sensitivity as any over several centuries. Where they are different is their starting-place, material and cultural; we shall return to this later.

As for the issues themselves, they are constantly present in society in one form or another. The war in Vietnam is horrible, but not uniquely so. The periodic bloodbaths that accompanied the spread of British hegemony in the 18th and 19th centuries elicited no such public antagonism, nor did the later extension of US influence to Cuba and South America and across the Pacific to the Philippines and beyond. Similarly, if it is the existence of racial oppression that has given rise to the Black Power movement, it is hard to see why this did not take place one-half century ago when the oppression was yet more grinding. If poverty and the inequitable distribution of wealth provide the mainspring of socialist movements today, there was still more scope for them during the period of naked industrial expansion in the late 19th century or during the Depression. (There were movements, but none with the broad base of support that the radical movement in the US now enjoys.) If economic exploitation of the Third World initiated mounting attacks on the great corporations, it provided a stronger reason before the Second World War, when companies like the United Fruit Company and Anglo-Persian Oil virtually ran whole countries for their commercial profit.

Issues are not the originators of change, but they provide the point on which the lurking passions of the day can focus. The First World War was not "caused" by the assassination of Archduke Ferdinand at Sarajevo any more than the Second World War was "about" Hitler's invasion of Poland. These wars were motivated by the threat posed to the integrity of other countries by the expansionist ambitions of Germany and Japan. But those events – the assassination and the invasion – happened when the underlying stresses had built up to a point when little was needed to release them.

2. Even if universal education has fallen short of what Victorian idealists hoped from it, it is still a powerful force for change. The nineteenth-century Utopianists looked for a new age in which men, freed by

education from the fetters of ignorance, would be able to exercise their full powers; the brutish mob would disappear, to be replaced by rational and responsible individuals. Perhaps the answer to the failure of that dream lies not in the innate irrationality of people but in the fact that they have been less "educated" in a true sense than subjected to a crude legal requirement that between the ages of 7 and 16 years they stay in institutions called schools.

Nonetheless the simple fact that most people can read means that they can have access to other people's thoughts from a wider range than was possible through social interaction. And even though much of the teaching comprises a sort of indoctrination with national myths – in Britain the myth of a glorious royal and imperial past; in the USA the myth of an unending struggle for national and personal freedom – these myths can themselves be inconvenient. The Victorians accurately saw universal education as potentially revolutionary, and the Tory party opposed it on those grounds.

Closer to home is the recent development of more widely available college education. In Britain and Europe only a small part of the population can hope to go on to further education; in the USA nearly one-half of the school-age children can hope to. Such a movement is justified on the grounds of providing equality of opportunity for the individual, needed skills in an increasingly technological age, and also – a belief which is rarely questioned – more of something which everybody tacitly agrees to be a good thing. But at the same time, as the ferment on the campuses showed in the 1960's, it forms large communities of young people away from their homes and the standards which ruled their behavior into adolescence. Perhaps for the first time, the students have freedom to experiment with unfamiliar modes of behavior and to question the assumptions under which they have been brought up. However, this cannot be a complete explanation. Such communities have existed before. And while students have always been rowdy and ungovernable they have usually, in the end, conformed to the expectations of society. We need more than the simple fact of more widely available education to explain the disaffection of students with established society and their willingness to set up a new culture in opposition.

3. In his book *Future Shock*, Alvin Toffler attributes great importance to technological change as the driving force of changes in society. He describes, for example, the greatly accelerating rate at which man can

travel. It is clear that cheap and rapid travel has changed the boundaries of people's lives, as compared with a time when the boundaries of a man's world and the circle of his acquaintance was set by the distance he could walk in a day. Mass communication does the same thing, "bringing the world into your livingroom" as the news shows have it, and providing access to a far wider range of models against which to measure our lives. The standards for what is "normal" are set by the houses, furnishings, and style of life of situation comedies like *The Lucy Show* or soap operas like *Peyton Place*. They come from a never-never land of folk myth, Frank Capra movies, and the world of admass. Yet they become the solid reality against which people from the East Side to Middle-West farming communities measure themselves. The boy from the farm no longer has to go to the big city to discover discontent.

By breaking down what are in some senses natural barriers and groupings, television and travel have removed the insulating distance between ourselves and events. We observed earlier that the Vietnam War is horrible; it would be less obviously so to individuals in the West if it were not happening in our living rooms. In this way efficient communications supplement the broadening effect of education. In the global electronic village everyone is a neighbor; we have access to and are involved in a wider range of experience.

4, 5, and 6. The next three categories fall together. Large groups are made necessary by — and make possible — a rapid increase in population. The city is a counterpart to the giant corporation, which must have a secure supply of workers (who want to be cheaply housed) and be within reach of supporting industries, also needing workers. Just as a corporation devises methods of organization to handle the problem of coordination, so does the city devise rules to handle problems arising from large numbers of people — problems ranging from the disposal of refuse, to parking laws and one-way streets, to planning restrictions and providing policemen. In both cases the stability of the system is maintained only through a high degree of specialization. In the company the activities of employees are rigorously defined and limited, subordinating them to the health of the system. The individual's complex capacity to perform many interrelated functions is pared down to the highly efficient performance of one. The cost of high population is borne more in loss of opportunity through limitations of resources: the opportunity to drive, dawdle, and sit where he likes, and the chance to live where he wants and in the way he wants.

These models of living and working are set in contrast to unattainable ideals: the arcadian ideal of life in unlimited space, and the preindustrial (almost Jeffersonian) ideal of complete and satisfying jobs within a small working unit. I call them unattainable not just because the world cannot support such a way of life for an increasing population, but also because cities, big corporations, and specialization of work have made possible a material standard of living which could not be attained in other ways. Assume that people want the standard of living and the rest will follow.

7 and 8. The last two categories also fall together. The authority structure within the family is faithfully mirrored in religion. The rights of a father to obedience are sanctioned and supported by religious precept — indeed, they are enjoined. Is the decline in religion, then, a function of the decline in the firm hold of the family? If the family that prays together stays together, the modern urban industrial family seems to do neither. And, of course, the interpenetration of systems goes further than that. According to the traditional rules, a good son was likely to be devout; he was also a good worker, tireless in pursuit of his duty to his employer, hardworking, and obedient. The standards of behavior, comportment, and dress were similar within all three systems. The priest could expect that his congregation would turn up soberly dressed on Sundays; an employer could demand similar restraint; fathers told their sons to cut their hair and clean their shoes. To conform was to display the recognition signals proclaiming that one was a member of decent society. Failure to conform was to run the risk of social ostracism, a socially disadvantageous marriage, and reduced prospects of promotion (the American myth of the "good rebel" notwithstanding). Yet today attendance at church has dwindled to little more than a social ritual; fathers are irrelevant past adolescence; and only in IBM do old rules of conformity in dress and behavior still apply.

I exaggerate. It is still a disadvantage for any political candidate to declare himself an atheist in America, and quite out of the question for a presidential candidate. (Even in irreligious Britain it is necessary for the Prime Minister to look pious on Sundays.) Companies other than IBM successfully insist on white shirts and dark suits. But there remains the question of why standards of behavior which at one time would have been regarded as eternal have been replaced overnight by others which would have seemed immoral. And it should be clear by now that the answer is not simple. Indeed, it is not even obvious whether any real distinction can be drawn between what are causes and what are effects. Both the decline of religion and the decline of the family have been nominated in their time as causes of social change, particularly of that group which includes sexual promiscuity, long hair, and drug-taking. But they are also the effects of changes elsewhere: the decline in religion, perhaps, of wider education and a more questioning attitude that had its roots in the Italian Renaissance; the decline of the family, in the growth of industrialization with its accompanying breakdown of rural patterns and the establishment of smaller family units in great conurbations.

It is impossible to establish clear causal sequences, let alone identify — as we attempted at the beginning of the chapter — single causes for complex social changes. I started by dismissing contemporary social and political issues from a more important role than that of seed crystal, essential as a starting point but not the source of power. Other nominees were seen to have more power for action but did not act alone; they have complex interrelationships with other systems which make them both the subject and the cause of change. The main point is that none of the suggested categories is exclusive: increases in the amount of education, technological advances, the size of companies and towns, the growth in population and specialization in work, the decline of religion and the family are all, to a far greater extent than I have sketched, complicatedly interlinked.

Nonetheless, I am going to suggest rather perversely that the direction of change has a coherence which is characteristic of a particular time, and that this coherence is given by the existence of an "enabling" mode of change. We intuitively feel that many of the movements which characterize social change today lean in some identifiable directions: towards individual freedom and self-realization, and away from codes of morals, social structuring, and authoritarian relationships. Such movement is in tension with the movements that have characterized the first part of the industrial development of the Western world — and to a large extent still do: towards the concentration of economic power, tighter integration within and between social and economic systems, and the subordination of the individual to the larger units of which he is a part. The rest of this book will be devoted to the thesis that the earlier patterns of change were the consequence of developments which have changed the balance of economic power within society and that this change has given rise to current directions of change. The enabling mode of change today is the rise in economic well-being.

SUMMARY

Companies must have some understanding of the likely directions of social change if they are to anticipate the effects within their organizations. It is difficult to establish simple causal relationships since there are many influences, all are interdependent, and all are concurrently the cause of some changes and the effects of others. The decline in religion, the growth of television, the breakup of the family, increasing affluence — these are all interrelated. The resulting visible social change is a product of shifts in the relationships between the underlying systems that make up society.

However, each period is characterized by a coherence in social change, a direction that comes from the existence of a leading or enabling mode of change. The dominant mode of recent history has been the integrative development of modern industrial economies. The result has been to knit groups into larger interdependencies, eliminating slack in the linkages at the expense of the individual. But this development has at the same time generated wealth which has conferred freedom of choice. And it is the effect of this freedom deriving from the rising tide of ambient wealth that is the enabling mode of today.

4
INCREASING WEALTH AND INCREASING CHOICE

If the ice-cap of Greenland was melted, I remember being told at school, the level of the seas around the world would rise by perhaps six inches. And the result would be the loss of huge tracts of land along the coastal strips of all the countries of the world. An inch or so more and yet more land would disappear: valleys would become inlets, plains become oceans, hills become islands. I always found it an oddly frightening thought; the effects seemed so disproportionate to the cause. It is no less frightening and disproportionate than the effects on society of quite modest increases in wealth. The tide of wealth is creeping up by fractions of an inch, and each advance is obliterating whole continents of inherited attitudes and accepted relationships. Our social landscape is being transformed. And this is being achieved by granting to the majority of people in the prosperous West two things, the secure expectation of the satisfaction of basic material needs and the privilege of choice, which revoke from the social systems the power to coerce their members.

Civilization is based on many forms of repression and coercion. It is part of the social contract that we repress, or abnegate, many basic and instinctual needs – in particular, sex and the spontaneous expression of feelings. Our behavior as children is shaped by the socializing process of growing up in a world where the rewards and penalties are in the hands of adults. When grown, our behavior is still subject to the often unspoken restraints of the systems to which we belong and from which we get our rewards. This much is so obvious as to be prosaic. However, the effect on the systems of coercion within which we operate is less clear.

At the most direct level, there is the effect on a man of changes in his job prospects. The difference between what managers could demand from their workers 40 years ago and what is possible now has complex roots, as we saw in Chapter 3. One change is straightforward: a man facing privation and a long period of unemployment as the alternative to compliance with his supervisors' orders is in a quite different position from a man who can walk down the road not only to another job but also to more money. One job is survival; two jobs to choose from is something like freedom. The change is felt in management too. The "natural" style of management in a hierarchical organization is authoritarian, and it is to be expected that managers will adopt this style when conditions permit. But once the managed are in a position to make their needs felt, a more persuasive — and ultimately more participatory — style becomes appropriate. MacGregor's "Theory X" set of assumptions may not be evil so much as more appropriate to conditions which are disappearing.

Our ability to see clearly this shift in the balance of power is confused when it is overlaid by moral precepts that derive from other systems. If hard work and obedience are given a moral value, as in the domainant Protestant ethic, the hard worker is seen as a "good" worker. When workers, responding to a shift in the economic balance, begin to exercise their power, they become "bad" workers and even "irresponsible," if they strike. These words do not help us to an understanding of the situation. It is hard to keep in our minds, for example, that a previous pattern of "responsible" behavior was enjoined within a framework that was able to impose heavy penalties for not conforming.

Henry Ford set up his assembly line at Dearborn in 1919 and paid his workers the unheard-of sum of $5 a day. His fellow employers were scandalized and muttered that Henry was selling the market system down the river; the Left was dismayed by what they saw as a move to subvert the coming revolution. But Henry was no liberal softie. He may have cared for his workers, but he also knew that his company would benefit from the well-nourished, loyal, hand-picked workforce that relatively high wages made possible. Moreover, he had stern ideas on morality, public and private. A team of women was established in the quaintly named

Sociology Department to ferret around for immoral, or merely undesirable, behavior – any of which was likely to attract fines. By the time the list of drunkenness, nonattendance at church, use of bad language, fornication, betting, and appearances at the pool hall had been compiled, the princely $5 had dwindled. Very few workers passed through the eye of Henry Ford's needle to their full wage.

This was a fairly naked use of economic power to consolidate the grip of value systems with which it was not in any necessary sense connected. That story could have been repeated many times in a period when privation and high unemployment gave great power to those in command of the reward system. The converse has followed: the economic balance has shifted through the accession of the countervailing power of unions and through fuller employment, and the power is no longer there. If Ford attempted to influence the private behavior of its workers today, General Motors would be very happy.

The rising level of ambient wealth is not a lone influence; as suggested in Chapter 3, there have been concurrent changes elsewhere – primarily in the broadening range of life models to which people have been given access through education and the mass communications media. But it has some force to act by itself. The level of crime in the USA, for example, is higher than in many parts of the world. However, visitors may be struck by the lack of coercive restrictions and control in many trivial things. People throw away roomfuls of furniture, where in other countries every scrap of waste, even down to tin cans, is preserved for other uses. Coathooks are screwed, not bolted, to the walls because nobody would bother to steal them. In some communities – the richer universities, for example – many of the basic goods like paper, pens, and even local phone calls are free goods. In a poorer society these goods are not free and the need to control them creates a structure that has the power to control small aspects of people's behavior. In this way the simple fact of a high level of ambient wealth in parts of US society creates a freedom that does not exist elsewhere. I am not suggesting that freedom in such small details will by itself lead to major social changes but merely that it is a component of change. Communists maintain that where all property is communally owned there can be no theft; where goods are free there is no need to steal them.

Bernard Shaw argued this case in a typically Shavian paradox in his play *Major Barbara*. He contrasted the benevolence of the arms manufacturer, Undershaft, with the work of his daughter, the Salvation Army

Major of the title. "Poverty is the only vice," Shaw argued; so that Undershaft, by providing wealth through employment in his prosperous business, was acting in a truly philanthropic fashion. Major Barbara, doling out bread and syrup to the poor in return for their compliance with the Christian values of society, was merely perpetuating an unjust social system, providing the well-behaved workers essential for its survival. Like any good propagandist, Shaw oversimplified. Society is far wealthier now than in his time, but the Good Life, lived by rational and decent men, is still far away. Appetites are a hydra-headed monster: cut off the gaping head of Poverty, and two more grow in its place.

Readers may be familiar with the hierarchy of human needs put together by the psychologist, Abraham Maslow. They range from survival and security, through social and affiliative needs, self-esteem, status, the need for independence and autonomy all the way up to what Maslow called "self-actualization," which has something to do with the satisfaction of the urge to create. He maintained that these needs can only be satisfied in ascending order, the satisfaction of a lower releasing a higher need. Wealth comes into the picture because the needs short of self-actualization can at least in part be satisfied through money. The purchase of a big house in the best part of town is more than the purchase of a roof; it also goes some way toward satisfying the needs for status and social affiliation. A great part of the advertising effort of consumer industries goes into associating products with these needs, so that the consumer is convinced that he "needs" particular goods because they will make him greatly admired, powerful, or sexy. Thus his needs are transformed into the imperative need to earn the money which he is convinced will satisfy them. The consumer becomes, in the most literal sense, the slave of his appetites, for the level at which he sets these needs imposes limitations on what he can do with his life. That favorite of pulp fiction, the poor-but-gifted man who is driven by an ambition to prove himself and marry the girl from the big house on the hill, is unlikely to satisfy his lifelong urge to become a harpsichord maker or a botanist.

It is because industry has been successful in building these elements into our personal patterns of demand that Professor Galbraith talks about the loss of consumer sovereignty to the point that it's now the producer who rules the market. This is true enough in the short term (if condescending — I wonder if such social commentators feel as ruled as they claim others to be) but not, I suspect, in the longer term. Consider three reasons:

1. As the absolute level of wealth rises, the importance to the individual (marginal utility) of each succeeding addition declines. And with it declines the power of the economic system to coerce its members through withholding its rewards. A man may risk death to feed his starving family, as many were forced to in the dangerous jobs of less trammelled times; he is unlikely to do so to buy his son a new bicycle.

2. The collective intelligence of society is a formidable instrument for filtering out the socially useless, in the long term. (In the short term, as politicians know to their cost, crowds are brutish and unruly.) And the more grotesque excesses of the consumer society — from the annual model change to vaginal deodorants — will be discarded, when they are not first banned by legislation. (Admittedly they will be replaced by others.) A more conscious expression of this sense of discrimination is the rise of consumerism.

3. The renewal of society by young people is constantly increasing the proportion of those, first, who have been brought up on a diet of advertising and are to some extent immunized and, second, who have been brought up with secure prosperity as the assumed background to their lives. They are not driven by the same needs as their parents.

The last point is clearly demonstrated in the gap between student and worker politics. One illustration sticks in my mind, experienced during my stay at MIT's Sloan School in 1969-70. The key issue for the students then was the role of MIT as a defense contractor, with particular focus on the place within the university of the Instrumentation Laboratories, heavily involved in the missile programs. In the Fall of 1969 a meeting was held between student radicals and workers from the Laboratories, and I wrote at the time:

> "The I-Lab workers spoke up for traditional patriotic virtues. And for their jobs. They were followed by SDS spokesmen who explained that they (the workers) were betraying their class by building bombs to drop on other workers. They should refuse. . . On the stage were the children of privilege, telling the workers to put their jobs at risk. They wore clothes that were symbolically torn and dirty (rejecting the values of bourgeois society) while around me were men whose clothes were torn and dirty from real work, men who wanted nothing more than the things the students were rejecting. . ."

Not that the students were wrong in rejecting a world of three-car families, color TV in all the bedrooms, and mink bedspreads, but they could hardly have expected the workers to follow them to a more austere life without first having experienced the sickly joys of overspend. (The world has always been full of unhappy rich men telling unhappy poor men that wealth does not bring happiness.) There was a gulf between the two groups, fixed by freedom of choice. If the students were poor and shabby, rejecting the bourgeois values of their parents, it was through choice. And when it was all over, the protests made, they could always *choose* to reach into the closet and take their suits out of mothballs. The workers did not have such choices. They were held no longer in the grip of the threat of privation but that of their mortgages and the urge to consume. The students were, even if only temporarily, free of these bonds. But then, students have always been freer than other groups in society. If they have not chosen to exercise that freedom as much in the past as presently, they have also been in the grip – or imagined themselves to be, which amounts to the same thing – of the systems from which they would seek rewards. How much this has changed can be seen in the Case of the Disappearing Engineering Graduate.

The shortage of engineers is a recurrent complaint of US industry, and although one may be skeptical about the real size of the gap, its reality is reflected in the starting salaries commanded by new graduates. According to the Engineering Manpower Commission, the median starting salary offered in 1969-70 to engineers ranged from $797 to $849 per month. In the same year liberal arts majors commanded a median $702 and pure scientists $784. This premium on engineers has been a consistent trend since the mid-1950's. Yet the market has not responded to the efforts of employers to elicit greater supplies with higher salaries. Quite the reverse: engineers have lost ground in the proportion of degrees awarded. In the ten years to 1968, the number of engineering degrees conferred rose by one-third while that of social science majors increased by two and-one-half times. Meanwhile, a number of estimates of the engineering manpower situation (from the employers' federation and government departments) have put the shortfall between supply and demand at between 10 and 25 percent annually.

A clue to this anomaly may lie in the apparent unpopularity of the engineering course and the ambivalence of engineering students to it. An attitude survey carried out in some Eastern colleges (for an unpublished

Master's thesis at MIT)* yielded significant differences between engineers and other students. Most striking was the response to the statement, "If I had it to do again, I would choose a different career." More than one-half the engineering students were neutral to strongly in agreement with the statement; none of the students in other disciplines registered a single vote of agreement. Second, there is a high rate of switching out of engineering: in the ten-year period referred to above, engineering majors accounted for 14 percent of the freshman intake but only 6 percent of final degrees.

The decision to study engineering has unusual features. Unlike other academic disciplines, it involves a virtual commitment to an industrial career; four-fifths of graduating engineers take jobs in industry. And it is a commitment entered into four years before it can become effective. However, it does carry some sort of guarantee of secure employment. For a young man looking ahead into an uncertain future, it may seem a wise and safe choice – in times of high unemployment, extremely so. But the cost is high in terms of preempting choices that the student may wish to make after leaving college. At the freshman level of knowledge, it is more natural to make a choice that leaves options open and that does not commit him for the rest of his career.

Even in the absence of changes in college attitudes to industry and in the range of job opportunities, the rise in the absolute level of starting salaries would probably have affected the behavior of the market. For the year 1969-70, the median starting salary of a liberal arts major was $147 a month below that of a chemical engineer. Nonetheless, he had $702 a month to live on. The difference is significant, but it is less so than the same difference would be at lower salary levels. We would expect that the sacrifice involved in choosing the lower-paid of two jobs would become less as the salaries involved increased, providing the differentials remained the same. The appeal of the engineers' high starting salaries declines, therefore, in relation to that of other occupations as the general level of salaries increases.

This brief sketch begs many questions about the nature of the market for graduates and the motivations of students in job choice. Nonetheless the failure of the market mechanism for engineering graduates can plausibly be said to contain the elements we have discussed, specifically:

*Chapman, David, and R.J.C. Roeber, "The Role of Student Attitudes Towards Industry on Job Choice," 1970.

- Increased choice among a greater diversity of job opportunities offering adequate salaries; exercised in the student's interests.

- Willingness to use that choice in the absence of constraining fears about job opportunities; changed attitudes toward business careers; the wish to keep options open.

This shift is, in fact, a very pallid reflection of the vivid changes that have taken place in universities during the sixties. But it is one of the forms in which the more visible changes present themselves to a business community that can no longer regard itself as bestowing favors with its jobs. I think it likely that the highly publicized manifestations of college disaffection with established institutions are less likely to bring about social change than are the more subterranean shifts in relationships which the case of the disappearing engineering graduate represents. By the same token, smaller increases of permitted degrees of freedom — as in choice of jobs from a limited range for the shop floorworker — carry far greater potential for change, because they are so much more widespread.

It would be a distortion to suggest that these changes have been brought about solely by increased wealth. As we discussed in Chapter 3, there have been a series of concurrent changes in other systems. But the increase in the level of wealth, seeping into the structure of society, dissolving and eroding, has been the enabling change. It has loosened the structure and enabled systems to shift into new relationships with each other, thus releasing the stresses in society. And wealth achieves this by bringing with it choice, a wider range of possibilities at each decision. Choice means questioning and evaluating alternatives, and this is profoundly revolutionary when the choice is exercised in the individual's interests. More than anything, it means that we are moving toward a "voluntary society" in which membership in the systems within society is by free choice and not imposed.

SUMMARY

Increasing affluence, or rather the wider range of choices that affluence makes possible, is the most revolutionary force at work in society today. The rising level of wealth is removing people from the rigid constraints of a society whose fundamental discipline is the threat of privation. It is generating some limited degrees of freedom of choice. People tend to exercise such choice in their own interest, resulting in the weakened power

good pts

of a social system to coerce the behavior of its members. This produces a move to a more "voluntary" society in which people are members and conform to the behavioral standards of only those systems to which they voluntarily commit themselves.

or groups

5
TOWARD A VOLUNTARY SOCIETY

To suggest that we are moving toward a society which will be in many ways freer than today's must seem perverse when it is so obvious to many people that we are headed in the opposite direction, into the world of Orwell's *1984*. The processes of economic and technological change continue, inexorably gobbling up the slack within and between systems, knitting them together into larger units and more complex interdependencies. The megamachine and megacorporation dwarf our tiny humanity; the databank robs us of privacy; manipulative persuasion robs us of choice and variety. The individual is strapped into the machine with only the freedom to consume and procreate within limits set for the convenience of the system before, like some broiler chicken, reaching his unimportant end. Thus we see the myth of man the victim of capitalism, according to our more apocalyptic commentators and the dogma of radical politics.

This is not altogether a myth, however. The processes of integrative change will not suddenly stop: corporations will continue to grow larger; the world is shrinking; the rate of change is accelerating. But within this framework, the area of self-determination around individuals is growing to a point where it may challenge the integrative changes. It is a counter-current of change, a reaction against loss of humanity which has itself been brought about by the wealth which that same loss once generated.

My view of the instrumentality of wealth in this change may arouse objections on the grounds that it is mechanistic. The more positively political and more romantic view is that such changes are enforced by the irresistible power of public will: the individual is rising to throw off his shackles, declare his faith in love and humanity, and, if necessary, by destroying the existing system bring society to its senses. The existence of a will to be free is, of course, a necessary condition of a purposeful move toward greater freedom. But I have assumed that this has always been present and that what has released it in our times is a slow shift in the underlying balance of power in society. The most rational and just demands for social change are ineffective if the energy for change is not present in society.

It is for this reason that I see the greatest force for change being generated where the will is most widespread, in the mass of the population, and not necessarily where the manifestations are most visible. A spark from the fire does less damage than a pan of boiling water although it has a far lower temperature. And the sparks, brilliant and intense, are to be found in the colleges, where the purest manifestations of the move toward voluntarism have emerged. This is the face of the new society:

> "Its foundation is liberation... the individual no longer accepts unthinkingly the personal goals proposed by society... it postulates the worth of every human being... members of it do not measure others. People are brothers and the world is ample for all... a community. In personal relationships, the keynote is honesty and the absence of socially-imposed duties... In this new society, people neither give commands nor follow them; coercive relations between people are wholly unacceptable. And they also reject any relationships based wholly on role, relationships limited along strictly impersonal and functional lines... Thus the new generation looks with suspicion on obligations and contractual relations between people, but believes that honesty can produce far more genuine relationships..."*

The description is culled, with emendations, from Charles Reich's catalog of the virtues of what he calls "Consciousness III" which appears in this book, *The Greening of America*. It is a life style which Mr. Reich sees as emerging in reaction against established systems, or perhaps the

---

*Reich, Charles, *The Greening of America*. New York: Random House, Inc., 1970.

next logical development of them. And it is the purest form of a working voluntarist society. (I exclude dropout communities for reasons we shall examine later.) But it is very much the product of the college environment within which students are almost completely protected from the rigors of "real life." Away from the need to shape behavior in ways that will elicit rewards from the system, they are free to construct an ideal society in which there are no such things as "working relationships." But in a world of work such honesty may not be possible since, unlike the college environment, the relationships are not freely chosen but the random outcome of the requirements of work. Faced with such realities, many of the purer forms of the new society will be extinguished, sparks falling into a puddle. But there will be an export of voluntarist ideas from college, however much they are modified once the individuals become enmeshed in the reward systems of established society. And there will be attempts, probably in increasing numbers, to establish communities such as communes where the new life style can be maintained – although, again, experience suggests that these are bound to have limited lives.

The most realistic assessment of the function of these college manifestations may be that of all extreme political movements. Society will never respond to more than a tiny part of any body of extreme political demands; the inertia is too great. But extremism sets up a model which is so dissonant with the accepted models of society that it forces a reassessment of them, even if only partial. For the more impatient, the natural route for these changes seems to lie in revolution.

However, organized political movements are not a central part of the move toward voluntarism, although some are logically related outgrowths. What is quite new about this pursuit of old needs and wishes is the lack of structure and its pervasiveness. There are no political parties, no sectional interests to balance, no program of action – just a steady sifting of choice into the population, the slow shift of power as that choice is used. The unit of action is the individual, for it is the individual who is being given the power to choose in many little ways. And given choice, he is using it in his own interest. Even if it grants to the individual only limited increases in his freedom, the effects are profound.

A. Probably the first of the shifts toward voluntarism which arose from economic changes and is continuous with the present moves was the whittling away of the family. This is an amply documented sociological phenomenon; many influences have been identified: the industrial revolution and the accompanying drift from agriculture to the cities;

breakdown of established "tribal" patterns with such large movements —
which includes, very significantly for the USA, emigration; the erosion of
the principle of authority; decline in religion. As we saw in Chapter 3,
none of these influences acts alone. However, the more recent phenomenon of almost complete dispersal of children past the age of puberty
would not be possible, whatever the other influences, unless they could
support themselves independently. Given choice, they exercise it in what
they see as their own interests and choose to escape the tyranny of home.
As countries industrialize and a wide range of jobs becomes available, the
centrifugal pressures on families grow until the family as an institution is
virtually dissolved.

B.   Closer to the present, we are in the middle of growing dissatisfaction
in industry which does not take organized forms — except the ritualized
form of regular pay demands by unions — but appears in disorganized
ways such as strikes, absenteeism, and high turnover. Industry responds to
the phenomena according to the old rules of "pay more and push harder"
but with decreasing success. It would be an exaggeration to say that the
entire system is facing breakdown; some parts of it, however, certainly are.
The troubles experienced by General Motors on its Vega assembly line in
Lordstown, Ohio, where there has been extensive malicious damage
resulting in heavy costs to the company, suggests that some radical changes
are needed.

C.   Less ambiguously, changes will be enforced because companies can no
longer find people to do certain jobs — another product of full employment. Among the first to go in an industrializing country are the servants;
in rich countries it is sometimes impossible to get domestic servants at any
price and perhaps one day it will be totally impossible. The result is a
change in the lives of the rich. Changes in industry are taking place
continually in response to an unwillingness to do certain jobs when other
work is available. The dyestuffs company referred to in Chapter 1 must
change or eventually go out of business; in areas where there is alternative
employment the coal mines in Britain are facing a loss of manpower that
could threaten even the most highly mechanized pits; the disappearing
engineering graduate mentioned in Chapter 4 is exercising his own freedom
of choice. In the seriously threatened industries radical changes will have
to be made to meet the new conditions; where the work is unpleasant and
of low status, it may have to be rethought if it is to be done at all.

D. The loss of an agreed moral base in society goes with the loss of authority. Where there is a consensus about what is "good" in society there is a power base for authority which is outside the sanctions of the economic reward system. But children question their parents' rights over them; students reject the authority of their colleges; workers reject the "divine rights" of managers; even in the army in Vietnam the right of superior officers to dictate is questioned. This rejection is seen as immoral by people brought up to value obedience. But obedience is not an absolute moral value. It provides an efficient means to an end, when the environment allows. When the conditions change, which they have, the requirement of obedience becomes inappropriate and some other means of eliciting the desired behavior must be devised.

E. In the voluntary society, fundamental assumptions are being constantly challenged. Choice requires questioning thought, and there are not many fundamental assumptions that can stand up to questioning. Thus the emergence of a "unisex" society — in which the roles of men and women are less sharply differentiated — is a result of questions about assumptions concerning the relative roles of the sexes. To wear hair long is perhaps to demonstrate rejection of the ethic that identifies manliness with brutality and exploitation, and that regards sex as a game in which the woman can only lose. The new "feminine" man rejects *machismo* as an impoverishment of the possibility of equal relationships between equal people. A change has been made toward a freer, more voluntary, less coerced relationship between the sexes.

F. This questioning extends into the most important parts of society — and nowhere is there more vigorous questioning than in the temple of the marketplace. Adam Smith's "invisible hand" has been found wanting, particularly by the young beneficiaries of the most developed and richest society the world has seen. They have grown up with plenty and it has no charms for them; they are too aware of the goods the market does not provide.

In his account of a protest march on the Pentagon, Norman Mailer describes a break in the proceedings in which sliced bread was offered round, "the comic embodiment now of a dozen little ideas, of corporation-land." He then goes on to draw a parallel between the mentality which makes tasteless bread for profit and also "at the far extension of the same process. . . was out in Asia escalating, defoliating. . ."

The point is not whether the insight is valid, but that it is part of a widespread disenchantment with the free market and all its works. The people Mailer described were not freaks, mutants, or subversive deviants. They are part of a new social system breaking cover, one of Emery's "emergent systems," characterized by a willingness to question and by a detached, skeptical freedom from the traditional values and norms of society. That the skepticism is often hostile and destructive we know from the events of the past ten years. More to the point of this section, it is a sort of questioning which does not see the logic of a system which produces, by the awful logic of the market, not better but worse goods.

G. Mailer makes the mistake, common in politics, of wrapping too many things in the same package for convenient blanket disapproval: somehow "corporation-land" ends up killing the Gooks while we, readers and author, who make up the corporations and pull the triggers, are somehow less involved. (Corporations do not exist in spite of but because of — and to serve the needs of — the people whom they oppress.) A more direct and meaningful attack on the assumptions of the marketplace is being generated within the consumerist and environmentalist movements, which specifically question and criticize those aspects of capitalism which are seen to be antisocial. Product design falls inside that sacrosanct area of managerial prerogatives which is being challenged inside the corporation. It is still the case that products evolve more or less blindly toward those aspects of design which the market responds to. Since the results are often inefficient, wasteful, and dangerous — because the market may not be sensitive to efficiency, proper use of resources, and safety — the consumer movement is developing other devices to make sure that social considerations are introduced. The environmentalist movement is, in my view, more complex since it touches deep-seated feelings about man and his relationship with the natural world. The issues are real, but the response to them is disproportionate in its energy and violence. And this suggests to me that the sources of energy are not the overt issues alone but involve something more atavistic or even superstitious. But whatever their roots, both movements represent another aspect of the new willingness to question and to choose.

H. Although I have stated that the movement towards the voluntary principle is nonpolitical, it has political manifestations. Consumerism and environmentalism are quasipolitical; Black Power and Women's Lib are more overtly so. And these, too, arise from the desire for more freedom, a larger area of self-determination, and the urgent need to decide for one's self who one is and on what terms one is to be a member of society. To be a black man in a white society is to have much of what "black" is to mean defined and handed over in a package at birth. The energy underlying Black Power derives from more than a demand for justice; it is an assertion that black men will have the right to decide for themselves what being black is to mean. ("Black is beautiful" is a highly significant slogan in a society where goodness and beauty are both white.) Women's Lib has less energy for action because there is far less tension in the underlying system: there are injustices, but there are also ancient means for redressing them. Nonetheless to be a woman in a man's world is also to inherit a specification which is limiting. Women's Lib is an assertion that the individual shall decide what being a woman shall comprise. It is ironic that in both these movements a sort of "neo-repression" is emerging as new definitions of "black" and "woman," different but no less restrictive than the old, are being worked out to the satisfaction of the movement.

I.   My last example of voluntarism — direct political action against the government — is further along, but not yet at the end of the political scale. I shall not dwell on it, since it is dominated by the intrinsic energy of the issues themselves, specifically of the reaction against the Vietnam War. The reaction is more than opposition to the war; it is a demonstration of the failure of the institutions of democratic government to provide a means through which the will of the population can affect decisions. Unless such a means is provided, there will be increasing numbers of campaigns by minorities to force their views on government. People may no longer be content to be ruled by the machine, without involvement in the decisions, any more than they are content to work without involvement in companies. Companies are changing many of the assumptions of management in response to this need; governments will have to change too, although they will move far more slowly and reluctantly.

These are some of the leading features of our emerging "voluntary society." The starting assumption is the existence within every man of a wish to be free to decide his own destiny, and the fact that society has held those wishes in check by a variety of means. The changes we have examined have been made possible by the relaxation of those social and economic constraints on individual wishes, specifically through the increase in the range of choices available to the individual. From the existence of choice comes the need to question.

Rationally exercised, this new freedom should lead to a truly free society: people would become voluntary, not coerced, members of society. But that is a long way off. The degrees of freedom I have discussed are small in relation to the whole range of individual wishes, but they are of immense significance psychologically. Only a very small minority, a few isolated groups, have anything near complete freedom of choice — the very rich, students, the very talented, or dropouts — either through having the power to buy or demand what they want, or through redefining their needs so that they fall within the limits set by the means available to satisfy them. (This last freedom is available to all who are not actually starving, but it is taken only by those whom society itself redefines as eccentric.) And even these few rarely feel as free as, in an objective sense, they are. The rest of us are relatively tightly constrained. But within those constraints there are now degrees of freedom where there once were none.

It is this small area of freedom around the individual that characterizes the move toward voluntarism. The unit of action is the individual, for it is to him that the power of choice is being given. In the short term it will force changes in working assumptions on many institutions — from government and industry to universities. In the longer term it raises questions for society itself.

The short-term adjustments are immense, since they will mean changes to forms of management — in and out of industry — which must elicit the voluntary commitment of the members. The degree of real or implied coercion that exists in a contract of employment will be replaced by a more equal relationship. (The effects on industry are the subject of the later part of this book.) The old coercions of teaching in the "good" schools will be replaced by teaching based in the assumption that students want to learn. These changes have been taking place steadily over several decades in industry and for a lesser period of time in universities. (Douglas MacGregor's "Theory X" assumptions would simply not have been questioned 40 years ago.) The changes in government will take longer; although they exist to serve the needs of the people, they have evolved in directions — particularly in the establishment of huge permanent departments — that make them largely impervious to popular pressures. But governments, too, will have to devise ways of eliciting the voluntary commitment of the population and of providing something like the reality of democratic administration. Ironically enough, the changes in industry could provide a model for changes in government: industry is more directly threatened and more responsive.

These changes are all in one direction, shifting power into the hands of individuals. Ideally in a voluntary society it would be possible for the individual voluntarily to abnegate his own needs where they conflict with that of the larger good. It should be possible to devise methods of working together that allow us to obtain the benefits of our highly complex wealth-creating sector without crippling and impoverishing the lives of the people who work in it. Thus if large units are a necessary part of our wealth, companies must make them places where human beings can exist. But at the same time, the workers must respect the basic nature of the machine. This compromise should be possible.

There is little sign among the young that they are prepared to trade away any of the new power, offering voluntary integrative change to offset the effects of disintegrative. Yet without a willingness to subordinate some parts of one's self to the systems of which one is a member, even a voluntary member, society cannot exist. We can only head into a world of pure play, the world of the Dionysian:

"Now the slave is free; now all the stubborn, hostile barriers which necessity, caprice or shameless fashion have erected between man and man are broken down. Now, with the gospel of universal harmony, each one feels not only united, reconciled, blended with his neighbours, but as one with him. . . In song and dance man expresses himself as a member of a higher community — he feels himself a god, he himself now walks about enchanted, in ecstasy, like to the gods whom he saw walking about in his dreams. He is no longer an artist, he has become a work of art. . ."*

The resemblance to Charles Reich's description of "Consciousness III," quoted at the beginning of the book, is obvious. It is the final statement of romanticism, in which the artist has become larger than his art until the work of art disappears altogether. Passmore comments that an attempt to base a society on play must lead either to collapse or to tyranny. In such conditions the revolution which I believe to be impossible today could well become possible. If a voluntary society is to remain free, its members will have to learn how to accept — also voluntarily — restraints on their freedom. Such restraints were imposed in the past, sometimes harshly; to learn how to live within them when they are not enforced, and to do this in the interests of society as a whole, would be an

*Nietzche, Friedrich, in John Passmore, *The Perfectibility of Man*, New York: Charles Scribner's Sons, 1971.

act of great social maturity. We have no alternative. Unless we learn to be mature, our society will cease to exist.

SUMMARY

The dissolving, loosening effects of choice — disintegrative change — are in tension with the integrative changes of technological and economic optimization. But they will continue to grant greater freedom to the individual within a framework of larger units and more systems integration. What will emerge will be a "voluntary" society. The purest form of this is found at the colleges, where students have a period of almost complete freedom in which to develop alternative life styles. But although they will exercise considerable influence, the purest forms are unlikely to survive in the open world.

The greatest change is coming from the massive accumulation of small elements of free choice throughout the population. The leading characteristic of the move toward voluntarism is its lack of structure and pervasiveness. There are many manifestations: the growing dissatisfaction of workers; the impossibility of getting people to do certain jobs or, if workers are hired, of being able to ensure that jobs are done well; the loss of an agreed moral base in society and the rejection of authority; the questioning of such basic assumptions as the relative roles of men and women; the rejection of the blind workings of the marketplace and, specifically, the attacks on market mechanisms by consumer and environmental movements; the more political movements like Black Power and Women's Lib; the dissatisfaction with a democratic process that provides no means for the will of the population to be effective in large decisions. These are manifestations of a willingness to choose and a need that this enforces to question.

But the change is in one direction, even though it is in tension with the forces of integration. And this is potentially gravely threatening to society. Unless individuals voluntarily learn to accept restraints on their freedom in the interests of society as a whole, it could cease to exist. The outcome could be chaos or tyranny — or the right conditions for a revolution.

6

CASE 1/ALLIED MINORIES: A Case of Organizational Change Triggered by Shifts in the Commercial Environment

BACKGROUND

1. Commercial

Allied Minories is one of the top five companies in its field in the world. It has a large international business with its main overseas markets in countries formerly under British influence. In Britain, where the case takes place, it employs 30,000 people.

The company had its origins in mergers that took place between the World Wars. Although the structure of the company changed, the component companies never quite lost their identities. The traditional pecking order between them – with its economic (profitability), social (class), and technical (intellectual) overtones – persisted as an influence on subsequent events.

A more important influence on management attitudes was the commercial environment in which the company grew. Before the Second World War, Allied Minories was virtually unchallenged within its chosen territories. Overt and covert cartels – of a sort standard in industry before the Second World War – buttressed by elaborate cross-licensing agreements gave the company a substantial degree of protection from competition in overseas markets and, with tariffs, almost complete protection in Britain.

The main constraints on the company's success were technical. In common with other technology-intensive companies operating in an absence of commercial pressures, the main focus of management attention was technical. Until the early 1960's the company's Board was dominated by engineers and scientists. In the prevailing economic climate the company had few problems with its labor force; Allied Minories was a "good employer"; but human problems were not accorded much attention by management.

This situation persisted even when conditions changed. After the Second World War the cartels and other agreements were dissolved. But acute shortages were experienced in almost all manufactured goods, and there were no overt commercial pressures. Management, labor, and plant were fully stretched throughout the 1950's to produce all they could without having to seek new markets.

Numbed by surplus demand, the company drifted through a period of transition in the labor market in Britain. Labor troubles were more easily placated than rigorously dealt with; the situation became not so much a matter of high wages as of feather-bedding. The unions pressed for, and got, higher manning ratios and management acceptance of restrictive practices and demarcation agreements. It is highly significant that the opportunity presented by the prosperous 1950's should have been used by the unions to pack the workforce. This fact is an entirely accurate reflection of the preoccupation of many British unions with the security of their members' jobs.

Toward the end of the 1950's reality began to break through this comfortable surface. Huge surpluses of capacity were poised over the markets, the result of overinvestment by other companies attracted into the industry by high profits. And led by a slight recession in the USA, the avalanche broke: by 1961, US producers were dumping their products all over Europe. Quite suddenly the industry became intensely competitive and freely international.

The result was to change altogether the commercial environment in which Allied Minories operated. No markets were safe; any producer, however distant, was a potential competitor. The attitudes of management, their orientation and composition, changed in response — but slowly. The shift away from engineering to sales and financial preoccupations together with the internationalization of the markets produced a more outward-looking stance. But there was a large element of inertia. Seniority remained a high recommendation for promotion, and the ranks of senior management were dominated through the 1950's and into the 1960's by men whose early experience was a positive impediment to an understanding of the problems the company was facing.

By the early 1960's the situation was serious. A number of surveys comparing Allied Minories with its main international competitors showed that it was two or three times overmanned in relation to them. Thus the company was extremely vulnerable to increases in wages, which after a long period of high employment were threatening. With the growing importance of international competition, it was a matter of high priority for Allied Minories to improve productivity.

2. Local Conditions

Allied Minories has factories all over the country, using a variety of technologies in a wide range of local conditions. We are mainly concerned with the following five factories and the numbers there employed: Caghampton (12,000), Duggeley (7000), Blackborough (3000), Withenden (1400), and Pondings (2200).

The first two operated in areas dominated by declining industries, casualties of the industrial revolution. Steel, shipbuilding, coalmining, railway workshops, and heavy engineering were the main industries. They had been prosperous in their time but were now depressed, overtaken by changing technology, new materials, and livelier foreign competitors. The local history since before the First World War has been one of high unemployment or at best erratic employment. One consequence is that the unions' main activities center on the defense of their members' jobs. Restrictive practices and demarcation (the reservation of particular jobs for specified unions), which are standard throughout the country, here assume a Byzantine complexity.

Duggeley has been in operation for some decades, and as a steady employer in an area of high unemployment the company commands some local loyalty. The average age of the workforce is more than ten years over that at Caghampton — in the same part of the country — and it includes many men with more than 30 years' seniority. Caghampton is quite differently placed. One of the most recent of the company's factories, Caghampton has attracted a massive investment in the most advanced plant; several of Allied Minories' operating divisions are present in its factory. Caghampton has a predominantly young workforce; it inspires little local loyalty.

Blackborough is one of the company's oldest sites, operating several processes. The area in which it is situated has had a long history of stable employment. The company is well-established locally but is not a dominating employer. The employment catchment area is somewhat isolated from the rest of industrial Britain, and the workforce tends to have deep local roots.

Withenden is something of an anomaly among the company's factories. Allied Minories in the only sizable industrial employer in the town, which is a market town for an almost entirely rural area. Thus there is no long industrial history, and the unions are not as powerfully established as elsewhere. Moreover, the factory is completely isolated from other industrial areas, even more so than Blackborough.

In Pondings Allied Minories is one of the less important employers. It is an area which has attracted technologically advanced industries such as electronics and aerospace companies. The factory was established at about the same time as Caghampton. The workforce, perhaps because of the background of high skills, is more adventurous and open to change. Table 2 summarizes these features.

Such local variations are significant since local union offices have considerable autonomy. And while any major changes in company practice had to be agreed centrally, the wishes of the national offices of the unions are not in practice binding on members. More than anything, this is a consequence of the informal union structure of shop stewards. Dealing with many of the problems arising on a day-to-day basis, these elected representatives of the men have more real power than can be handled from the union centers.

The difficulties of negotiation that arise when the appearance of power is with the formal institutions and its reality with the informal was the central preoccupation of the Donovan Commission, reporting on industrial relations to the British Government in 1968. The commission said:

"Many of those who conduct industrial relations are content with things as they are because the arrangements are comfortable and flexible and provide a high degree of self-government. Existing arrangements can be condemned only because these important benefits are outweighed by the disadvantages: the tendency of extreme decentralization and self-government to degenerate into

Table 2.

	Caghampton	Duggeley	Blackborough	Withenden	Pondings
Size (employees)	12,000	7000	3000	1400	2200
Established	1949	1921	1904	1938	1944
Local industry	Declining (heavy industry)		Light engineering	Agriculture	High technology
Employment history	Erratic employment		Steady	No tradition	Boom during war
Union stance	Defensive; rigid		Tough but open	Pliant	Helpful
Management stance	Divided mandarin		Traditional professional		Open

indecision and anarchy; the propensity to breed inefficiency; and the reluctance to change."

We shall see how true this was for Allied Minories; how all change, even when it seemed most manifestly in the interests of the workers, was sometimes bitterly resisted by the unions; how the real problem was not the changes in practice and procedures which were the subject of the talk and negotiation, but changes in attitudes; and how managers' attitudes, no less than other employees', became important.

3. Allied Minories' Industrial Relations

The company had long established the practice of making main agreements centrally, leaving the detailed implementation to be worked out at local level. The agreement current at the time the case starts – in 1966 – had been in operation since 1955. With subsequent adjustments and additions it had become extremely complex, allowing for a multitude of different grades and subgrades with different scales for skilled and nonskilled workers. In addition, a substantial part (25-30 percent) of the workers' pay came from the bonus scheme which was intended to provide an incentive but introduced an element of instability in earnings, where circumstances were beyond the worker's control. At the same time, it was so designed that it was impossible to reward certain forms of effort, particularly mental effort.

The scheme was based in job measurement, which is well suited to reward physical and repetitive work. But in the more modern plants the most responsible jobs required more vigilance and mental effort than physical work; indeed many dial-watching jobs would be most successfully accomplished when there was least apparently happening. The problem of how to reward such key workers (probably 20 percent of the workforce) had long taxed the company, but successive attempts to devise new schemes were unsuccessful. Instead, plant managers were forced to condone distortions in the rules of job measurement to provide a measure of incentive reward.

That the system was becoming unworkably complex and unsuited to emerging conditions was the main – and politically crucial – justification for reforming the pay structure. A committee was set up in 1965 to examine these issues, and it received its main support from managers who hoped for a solution of the problems. There were also other strands which by themselves would not have led to action but which under the "disguise" of reform were to exercise influence on the committee's deliberations. These were:

Ethical Considerations. The company had a long tradition of being a good employer, which is to say better than the industry norm. Management prided itself on its ethical treatment of workers. One particularly difficult problem was the differential maintained between salaried staff and wage-earners. Staff were entitled to many fringe benefits — sickness benefits, holidays, pensions and the like — which were effectively a handout to a privileged section of employees. A more fundamental differential existed between the security of an unvarying salary for staff and the insecurity of fluctuating weekly wages for wage-earners. The differences could only be explained in terms of class distinctions and had long troubled the company's more thoughtful managers.

Behavioral Science. The work of behavioral scientists in the USA, particularly that of Douglas MacGregor, was becoming known. Among the few familiar with this work, traditional assumptions about the roles of workers and managers were being challenged. The committee's deliberations provided an opportunity to weave some of these ideas into the fabric of the new pay structure.

The final recommendations proposed radical changes that went beyond reform in Allied Minories' pay structure and probed deeply into underlying issues of motivation as well. The main elements were:

Organization and Manning. Flexibility in working to be introduced between unions; more rational use of workers; more self-supervision; fewer supervisory personnel.

Payment Structure. All employees on "staff" basis at annual rate, paid weekly; simplification and rationalization of grading structure.

The recommendations were cast mainly as changes to the pay structure but contained elements of the ethical and behavioral strands to which we have already referred. Some of them served several purposes. Thus "staff" status was both an inducement to the unions (an improvement in conditions and security) and the elimination of the old inequity. Changes in the supervisory side were cost-cutting, but could not be achieved without enlarging the responsibility of the workers. "Flexibilities" between unions would allow the design of more complete jobs.

After consultation with the managers of operating units, the company's Board approved the recommendations and gave the go-ahead for

discussion with the unions. There ensued a six-month period of negotiations, the first three months of which were taken up with securing the
unions' agreement to negotiate. Mistrust was rampant. The unions started
with a straightforwardly bargaining stance: they were interested in getting
more pay for their members; behavioral and ethical aspects were
contemptuously dismissed as window dressing. The company negotiators
were not prepared to give away more than was required to achieve their
own ends. Their objective was to secure changes in working practice that
would yield savings. Through some paper studies, the committee had
estimated that labor savings of up to 25 percent might be achieved. The
negotiators were empowered to offer two-thirds of the savings in the new
pay deal as an inducement to accept other changes.

The main obstacle was the issue of demarcations — the relinquishment
of tribal laws that ruled the workplace, allocating jobs and power between
unions. The unions were deeply threatened by the proposed loss of the
small security these demarcations offered. But eventually (after the first
three months) the union negotiators were persuaded of the company's
good faith, and in 1966 the Agreement on Pay Reform and Productivity
(APRAP) was signed.

THE CASE

APRAP embodied most of the principles of the committee recommendations. It also drew up a schedule under which the agreement was to be
introduced factory-by-factory through the company. The five works
already mentioned were nominated as the leading edge of this change,
experience gained in them to be progressively used in introducing APRAP
elsewhere.

So far the negotiations had been secret. Local union offices knew
informally that something was happening. Nothing official was said until
the launching of the agreement in January, 1967. This was carefully
coordinated in order to avoid any suggestion that local managers were
being given information that might put them at an advantage over local
union officials. Thus the agreement was scheduled to reach all members of
the company (even those not involved) at the same time. But the most
important part of the exercise could not be anticipated. In a note issued to
senior managers at the time, three points were made:

1. The initial step in any manning study had to be an analysis of the
   management structure. (That is, the management was as much in the
   target area as the shopfloor workers.)

2. A major training exercise was needed if the right people were to be found for the jobs.

3. The changes would only be successful if progressive attitudes were adopted *at all levels* in the company.

Change in attitudes remained the central activity of APRAP introduction — even though the procedural aspects and the numerous skirmishes with unions were more conspicuous. And this started with detailed discussions on APRAP, led by experts from the central personnel office.

Discussion was needed. The initial reaction, from managers and shop stewards alike, was incomprehension. The changes proposed were too radical and disruptive of existing patterns to be easily absorbed. Understanding only came slowly, as managers, shop stewards, and finally workers worked through the agreement together.

Discussion was the main agent of change, with the management first explaining what the agreement was about. Later, teams of job assessors went through every job with the workers, management foremen, and shop stewards involved. Initially, the managers had to gain an understanding of the need for change, and they used the same arguments — about the company's commercial situation — that were used at the beginning of the exercise. Once a measure of acceptance had been achieved, the discussions went more deeply into the sort of change that might be relevant. Thus building up the picture of change through interchange with the people most concerned, everybody gained ownership of the resulting proposals. But in practice it did not always work that way.

In Withenden and Pondings this process yielded some useful results. In the other plants the response was more direct, particularly from the shop floor. As one shop steward put it: "The fellows looked through to see where the money was. There wasn't much for them and they weren't interested." However, at Blackborough and Duggeley there was at least a willingness to talk about the agreement. In some plants at Caghampton, led by their highly militant shop stewards, the men queued up to throw the agreements into the furnaces. This was an apt enough symbol of the defensive stance taken by the unions at Caghampton, rooted in a deep suspicion of anything that came from management in general and from central offices — all central offices — in particular.

At Caghampton, Duggeley, and Blackborough, the resentment at having an agreement sprung upon them was one of the main obstacles to be overcome in gaining voluntary acceptance of it. Local unions felt that something was being imposed from London by "them" — management and national union executives alike. Shop stewards, on whose cooperation much depended, felt this most strongly. They were accustomed to a large measure of responsibility for local union affairs and felt excluded by lack of consultation. "Why should we care? Nobody asked us what we wanted." was a fairly typical response.

The managers at factory level had their own substantial personnel departments which handled local responsibilities. They were also resentful but, as part of the management structure, less articulately so. As APRAP negotiations proceeded, they were to insist that they could have done better if they had been left to make separate agreements, and that the company as a whole had been forced to pay a high price to buy out the militants at Caghampton. (The dominating advantage of central negotiation was power-political: it was in the unions' interests to negotiate centrally since decisions on pay agreements were an important source of their national strength; the company negotiated centrally to avoid the probability that the unions would pick the factories off, one after the other, the concessions gained in weak areas being used as a precedent elsewhere.)

The initial responses provided an accurate indication of what was to follow. At Withenden the unions were not strong and management influence, exercised through supervisory levels, was important. Pondings was, as we shall see, a special case; the unions were strong there, but cooperative. At Blackborough, where there were strong unions rooted in a long history of local industry, the initial response was tough but there was enough trust between management and shop floorworkers in the relatively closed community for communication to be maintained. At both Caghampton and Duggeley there was an initial refusal to talk at all. But differences between the two factories emerged within a few months. The long history of Allied Minories' presence at Duggeley and the presence of long-service employees meant that, although the unions' attitudes were defensive, shop stewards had trust enough in their managers to discuss the agreement. But at Caghampton there was a complete refusal to discuss the agreement at all for three years. Other contacts were maintained, but no discussion on APRAP. These differences of behavior were to resolve themselves into regularities that could be related to:

1. Size of site. Management at the large factories encountered problems that were orders of magnitude more intractable than those encountered at smaller factories. These difficulties were probably a function of the political forces generated within large bodies of shop stewards, and of the difficulties of communication within a large site.

2. Location. Where the local industrial history was one of unemployment or irregular employment in declining industries, the unions' attitudes were more defensive than in prosperous areas. Where the sites were geographically isolated from other major industrial employers, communication within the workforce was less confused by "noise" generated outside.

3. Split management. At some of the larger factories, a number of plants with interlocking processes operated side-by-side but with allegiance to different product groups in the company. The plant managers had to make judgments between the demands of the factory and the product group. Since these were sometimes in conflict, plant managers usually favored the product group which controlled their personal reward systems.

The result of these growing differences was that the small factories at Pondings and Withenden were the first to "go on" APRAP in February and April, 1968. This expected and seemingly simple difference in behavior was, however, confused by another variable: the style of the local manager. The factory manager at Pondings had an almost evangelical zeal for the principles underlying APRAP. He worked tirelessly organizing meetings, arguing long into the night with recalcitrant shop stewards or managers. By his own enthusiasm, he communicated an enthusiasm for the principles of work-sharing, job enrichment, and participative decision-making which sustained — and to some extent still sustains — a spirit of dedication in the factory. At Withenden the factory manager was an altogether more solid type but a convinced believer in open communication within his workforce. His response to APRAP was a dismissive: "That? I've been doing it all my life." Thus in addition to the favorable local characteristics of isolation and small size, he had already — as a function of his personal style — established open relations with shop stewards and junior managers through regular meetings and frequent contact.

In both Pondings and Withenden the improvements in costs and productivity far exceeded the expectations of the central management — a fact that was to be important later when APRAP seemed to be foundering.

The manager at Blackborough encountered more opposition from the unions than did the managers at Withenden and Pondings. In style he was something of a traditionalist; "strict but fair" might be his description of his own standards. And he was a meticulous planner. Without the zeal of the Pondings manager, he nonetheless worked through the obstacles that arose from the managers and shop stewards with great thoroughness and hard work. The form of his activity was mainly meetings — to discuss problems, to define problems, to try to isolate what feelings were in the way of introducing APRAP, to list features of some other more ideal agreement. The unions at Blackborough accepted the agreement in November, 1968.

The experience at Caghampton and Duggeley was far more difficult. There, management style was completely swamped as a factor by the dynamics of the local politics. At the most extreme this meant the presence at the Caghampton factory of the dominating, militant, and highly political Barney McTavish, a senior shop steward with considerable influence within the factory and a determination to wreck any agreement coming from management. The problems at Caghampton for a time resolved themselves into the problem of McTavish. More basically, they were the problems of the large factory; of an alienated workforce which felt no sense of connection with Allied Minories; of a locale which had a long and bitter history of privation; and of unions, in response, that fought like tigers for their members' jobs — and saw very little else.

More than anything else, the opposition to APRAP was an opposition from the crafts unions. General workers' unions had little to fear and much to gain from the agreement, since it promised them more work. But the demarcations provisions struck at the very heart of the crafts unions' reason for existence. Demarcation represented jobs for union members in areas where jobs were scarce. The engineers' unions had to insist that the only workers allowed to use tools were their members — since not to do so meant handing jobs over to other unions. Thus even so trivial a job as removing a guard over a piece of machinery had to wait for an engineer to come along with his "mate" (unskilled assistant) and use the monkey wrench. The engineers would wait while the repair was effected — which could involve electricians and plumbers, all waiting for their turns at the one job — before replacing the guard. Meanwhile the general worker would have been waiting to resume his own job.

This hunger for jobs drove the local unions into maneuvers of considerable complexity. Thus it was the electricians' job to replace light bulbs — something that all the men did every weekend at their homes. At Caghampton the electricians' union was on the point of accepting that general workers could replace light bulbs when work measurement revealed that 12 jobs were involved. As a consequence, they refused. At another Allied Minories factory, the engineers insisted that filling soap dispensers in the mens' washrooms was their job, since it involved the use of a specially shaped key.

More fundamentally, the crafts unions – engineers especially – were struggling against a shift in the balance between the unions which was being brought about by technological change. As the plants grew more complex and expensive, the responsibilities of the general workers were increasing. But traditionally, the crafts unions, whose members had served long apprenticeships, were the "aristocrats" among the working classes. It was hard to accept the change in status, in work and out of it. And the analysis of work, the drawing up of job descriptions that lay at the heart of APRAP introduction, threatened to do just that.

Negotiations stuck at Caghampton and Duggeley. By the end of 1968 it became clear that APRAP was getting nowhere. Indeed, it was becoming a positive danger. The agreement provided a center around which a movement of militant shop stewards was coalescing – organized by McTavish. Whatever the real merits of the agreement, it had become a symbolic target and would have to be killed, or at least replaced, before it damaged the company.

A committee of Allied Minories directors was set up to consider progress on APRAP in January, 1969. They decided that the company had no alternative but to find other ways to travel down the same road: only radical changes in the methods of work could assure its long term survival; no return to the older methods would succeed. APRAP was to be killed and another agreement made to replace it. To break the deadlock in Caghampton and Duggeley, the committee recommended that all savings from the new systems of working be passed onto the workforce.

It was an optimistic decision, considering the problems the company was having. But the committee was strengthened in its recommendations by the experience of what could be achieved under more ideal conditions, as at Withenden and Pondings.

A new agreement was made with the unions. This time, with the valuable lessons from APRAP's mistakes, the approach was different. There was no secrecy. The unions solicited suggestions from local offices, the company from local management; the draft agreement was circulated to all employees to elicit further reactions and feedback. The modified agreement – the Pay and Staff Status Agreement (PASSA) – was not much different from APRAP. But it had a different name; it had been put together through a more cooperative effort; it was not sprung onto a surprised and resentful workforce (and management). And it contained concessions to crafts unions that were, arguably, to weaken the original conception.

The process of modifying the old agreement also provided an

adventitious means for overcoming the blockage at Duggeley. Negotiations had reached an impasse by the middle of 1968, and no progress was being made. Both sides were sticking to their points of principle – the management's based on the need to make APRAP pay, the unions' based on the need to safeguard their "birthright." But during the PASSA negotiations, and after a lengthy period of silence (consciously contrived by the management), the personnel manager responsible for APRAP asked for a meeting with shop stewards. The management and stewards were ready to talk; reasons for the blockage were listed and discussed; a number of key "sticking points" were identified and passed, without comment, to the central management negotiating team. These were substantially incorporated into the company offer during negotiations and the Duggeley talks got underway again when the modified agreement was accepted.

Managers responsible for APRAP at the five involved works met just before PASSA was signed, in order to pool their experience from APRAP and better evaluate the next step. The main headings from the resulting report were:

1. The first priority had to be *management education*. The agreement was in the hands of managers, and "there could be no sensible start to making it work until they knew what they were doing."

2. The group agreed that a single *failure in trust* between unions and management could "put back discussions and attitudes almost incalculably." Distrust of management's motives was universal. But the managers agreed that risk-taking actions – such as sharing company information which would normally have been regarded as too sensitive, in order to achieve greater understanding – almost invariably were repaid with trust.

By now the APRAP experience could be seen not only as an attempt to apply an agreement, but also as a process of education in the underlying principles. It had been the center of discussion for two years. The attention given to it in the first works had served to educate the rest of the company, particularly management. For the workers, the extra money offered remained the dominant concern. But the experience at Pondings and Withenden showed that a more committed attitude was possible and beneficial for all concerned. It was necessary first to gain agreement and then for the management, with supervisors and shop stewards, to make it work.

PASSA was signed in July, 1969. It was another year and one-half before the last factory in Allied Minories was "on." The problems encountered were similar to those briefly described for the first five factories. Again the key was to convince the workers of the need for change, the company's goodwill, and the real benefits — extending far beyond the extra money — which would result. This required breaking through the defensive attitudes of tradition (based in a justified suspicion of management's actions). And this was by definition a hard job: part of the agreement was the restoration of management prerogatives; and it was management trying to restore them.

As described, the negotiations surrounding PASSA provided an opportunity for breaking through the refusal of the Duggeley shop stewards to consider acceptance. With their example before them, the workers at Caghampton were soon pressing their shop stewards for a change. (The plants were in the same region.) But it required the successful handling of a strike by a new manager to gain the support of plant managers at the factory; and it took the dismissal of Barney McTavish — who predictably overstepped the mark, and lost even the support of his own members — to persuade the Caghampton shop stewards that their power was not limitless. Once discussions had been started, it was not long before the eagerness of the workers for the better pay rates overwhelmed any residual reluctance on the part of the unions.

CONCLUSION

The Allied Minories case describes a company's conscious and constructive response to changes in its environment. It was a change which grew more complex as it proceeded since the full extent of changes needed to reduce dissonance between the company's internal organization and the demands of its commercial and social environment was not perceived when the changes were started. The response came late but it was positive in the sense that it was in a direction designed to secure the company's long-run health and profitability. It marked the recognition of a transition in the environment which made former assumptions, structures, and values inappropriate.

As the dominant company in its chosen markets, Allied Minories had grown up in an environment which was in some senses protected. The management evolved to meet technical demands; commercial considerations were secondary, provided cost constraints were met; the human environment could be treated as a "given" and demands from the workforce were not a key constraint on management decisions. Not unnaturally, management had grown to accept that technical problems were the key constraints on the company's commercial success.

A number of complex, interlinked changes took place in the period between the end of World War II and the start of the case. The management only responded partially, to those aspects of change which experience and training had defined as important and which were accepted at a less conscious level as important in the company's managerial culture. Thus the company successfully adapted itself to changing technology, often leading the way in innovation. But with its eyes elsewhere, the management failed to identify — still less respond to — changes in the human and commercial environments, some of which were generated by that changed technology. Specifically, larger and more complex plants demanded more skill and intelligence from the operators running them; bigger single units and improved transport technology meant that old definitions of market boundaries were no longer relevant; affluence, education, television, and the increasing power of unions were resulting in a more demanding workforce.

The unconscious — or rather, unthinking — response of the company to these changes was to act in ways that tended to restore the status quo. This was possible because the generally high level of demand for the company's products during the 1950's insulated senior management from the effects of a changed commercial environment. Similarly, given the high level of activity, the need to maintain production was given priority over a rigorous examination of the long-term implications of union demands, which were more easily bought off, or acceded to, than responded to imaginatively. It was not until the company entered a period of commercial crisis at the end of the 1950's that any of these changes impinged on management decisions and the need to adapt to them was recognized.

The company faced two choices: continue to patch and replenish the old ways of doing things or face the implications and demands of the new changed environment. The company chose the latter course, although the choice did not present itself so starkly at first. Instead, managers agreed on the limited need to reform the wage structure and manning practices, which compared poorly with those of major overseas competitors. But this proved to be a far more difficult and complex task than it had been assumed.

Changes in manning practices and the company's offer of changed working conditions (as part of a productivity package) impinged on values and attitudes in the workforce. The request for cooperation and participation in discussions about new manning methods were in direct opposition to the ancient assumptions about "two sides" of industry and the inevitability of conflict between management and workers. The offer of annual salaries paid regularly — a major company concession — hit at a traditional way of life implicit on fluctuating pay based on hourly rates. Moreover, as a further complication, this fine structure of reaction to the change program varied crucially between factories in ways that seemed to derive from local history, culture, politics, and the technology.

Some but not all of these complications were foreseen when the changes were initiated. It was not to be expected that the full richness of response could have been cataloged at once. Instead, the process took the form of an untidy nest of change sequences set off by the "unfreezing" commercial crisis. A major framework of solutions was proposed in the initial package, which turned out to be incomplete but led to further unfreezing crises as it was worked out at a detailed level. These fed back and were instrumental in modifying the initial agreement.

Because of the local variations the extent of achieved change varies across the company; but the result, although far from the hopes of the agreement's originators, has been to change many internal assumptions about worker-manager relationships. The company is now set on a path which leads towards the development of constructive ways of dealing with conflict. How far the company and its employees can proceed down that path will be limited by the stability of managerial attitudes internally and of union attitudes externally. The latter will probably present the most severe limitation. Apart from the fact that managerial attitudes are to some extent within the control of the organization, the changes proposed are deeply threatening to the traditional role of unions. The problem is not confined to Allied Minories. As other companies make their adjustments, the unions will find themselves increasingly fighting yesterday's battles. In turn they too will have to decide whether to make changes in their organization to adapt (if it is not already too late) or risk becoming redundant for the purposes of representing their members' best interests.

SUMMARY

Allied Minories has for many years dominated its domestic British market and has a strong position in what was once the British Empire overseas. Overcapacity developing worldwide in the late 1950's led to a spate of dumping in the early 1960's which destroyed traditional areas of dominance and brought prices to low levels. The company was forced to consider its position in relation to main international competitors. Comparisons showed that it was grossly overmanned. Further studies exposed inefficiencies and restrictive practices in the labor force, conditions which had been known and tolerated in easier times but were quite inappropriate in the new situation. These studies culminated in a decision for a major reform of the pay structure and methods of working, and led to pressures to reassess management and union practices. In this way the original shifts in the commercial environment became transformed into an organizational change program.

The means chosen was a centrally negotiated pay agreement which was to be locally introduced. The agreement, made with national officers of the unions, offered more money and better conditions in return for more efficient manning practices. Specifically, the company offered a regular salary ("staff" status) in return for increased flexibility of working between unions. It was all to be negotiated in detail at the factories.

The agreement, known as APRAP (Agreement on Pay Reform and Productivity), encountered strong opposition from local unions and particularly from shop stewards; it also met with varying degrees of enthusiasm on the part of management. The shop stewards resisted the agreement on principle, because it had been reached without their participation. They further resisted for the more fundamental reason that the agreement constituted a threat to long-standing practices which, however restrictive they seemed to rational outsiders, represented jobs for their members. Resistance from management was not strong. Traditionalists disliked the loss of management prerogatives; junior management down to foreman level disliked the loss of responsibility that went with job enlargement for the workers.

The extremes of experience were widely spaced. In two factories there was virtually no discussion about APRAP for three years because of the shop stewards' refusal to talk. In two others the agreement was introduced and put into effect with considerable enthusiasm. It seemed that the main determining factors of these variations were the local environment and the size of the factory. Where there was a long history of erratic employment, the union attitudes were quite rigid; where the factories were large, there was a marked alienation between the company and the workforce and a strongly "political" body of shop stewards. There were also important differences between the attitudes of the unions: the most threatened were the most obdurate.

However, in several cases it was the impatience of the workers which finally broke through the procrastination. Not having the political involvement of the stewards, they were less committed to preserving union practice — except in the unions that stood to lose. As a general rule they were more open to change than their representatives, and far more enthusiastic about the possibilities that the new patterns offered for interesting work. Extra pay was the main consideration initially; bigger, more diverse, and more responsible jobs became more important with experience.

The agreement brought about useful overall improvements in manning, ranging from quite dramatically good in some factories to nearly negligible in others. But it did not achieve all that was hoped for, which was a structure in which organic improvements could be continuously made. The degree of change both in managers and workforce had been underestimated, as had the effort needed to achieve it. However, the agreement was organic enough to allow Allied Minories to take the next step. More importantly, it has shown the company which are the next steps to take toward a better use of its human resources. But, as one manager said, "It is like changing society itself." And given the importance of local tradition and of unions in the communities, this is what the company has to achieve.

7
CASE 2/THE INTERNATIONAL OIL INDUSTRY IN THE MIDDLE EAST: A Case of Adjustment Within a Changing Political Environment

The oil industry has been increasingly involved in the Middle East since the discovery in 1908 of oil in Iran. This is not without good reason, for the Middle East, with two-thirds of the "free world's" petroleum reserves, is incomparably the richest source of oil in the world. Not only is it prolific, but Middle East oil is also extremely cheap to produce. Yet it has not driven more expensive sources out of existence, nor has its low cost of production been reflected in any substantial lowering in price. Quite to the contrary, the effect of the upheaval in relations between companies and their host governments in 1970-71 (and probably into 1972) has been substantially to increase the cost of oil to consuming countries. The industry does not answer only to the rules of the market; many of the most important decisions affecting it are made through negotiation between companies and their host governments. And the point where the bargain is struck is a measure of the balance of power between the two sides.

THE PRESENT

How naked this confrontation can be was shown by the events of 1970. On May 3, a bulldozer cut the pipeline (Tapline) that carries crude oil from Saudi Arabia to the Eastern Mediterranean. The Syrian government, on whose land the break occurred, refused to give permission for the line to be repaired on the grounds that it was liable to attack from Israeli forces – and Syria could not be responsible for the lives of the workmen. In fact, it was no secret that the Syrians were pressing for an increase in transit dues (which they later received) and were using the opportunity to apply pressure. Their action quite adventitiously put enormous power into the hands of the two other suppliers of crude to the Mediterranean, Libya and Iraq. This was still during the time when the closure of the Suez Canal (following the 1967 Arab/Israeli war) forced the shipment of a huge part of Europe's supplies via the long haul, around the Cape. The oil companies had been able to cope with this strain on the supply lines – mainly a strain on available tanker capacity – only by increasing production of "Mediterranean" crudes as rapidly as possible. At the time Tapline was cut, they were already facing a winter demand that would stretch supplies to the limit.

Four days after Tapline was cut Colonel Gadaffi, the 29-year-old revolutionary leader of Libya, ordered the oil companies to restrict production on the grounds that overproduction was harming the oil fields. By late summer the loss of Mediterranean crudes was running at a rate of 60 million tons a year, all of which would have to be made up from the Persian Gulf with a long haul around the Cape. This was, to say the least, inconvenient for the oil companies. To major companies with oil production elsewhere the disruption could be handled, although at a heavy cost. But to companies with no alternative sources, which included many of the "independents" operating in Libya, it was more nearly disastrous. It was with one of these, Occidental, that the Libyan government had chosen to open negotiations designed to increase its tax revenue through changes in concession terms. In September Occidental – by now under severe pressure from customers because of the effects of production restrictions – agreed to changes in its contract with the government, of which the two major features were an increase in income tax from a 50-50 profit split to a 58-42, and an increase in the posted prices on which taxes are calculated. In the following month the other companies operating in Libya followed suit with changes in their tax rates and posted prices.

The change in Occidental's concession terms had been used by the Libyan government as a precedent for imposing similar terms on its other concessionaires. The new conditions in Libya were in the same way used as a precedent at the meeting of the Organization of Petroleum Exporting

Countries (OPEC) that followed shortly thereafter in Teheran in January, 1971. As a result of that meeting the concession agreements in the major exporting countries were all changed to the 55-45 profits split, and posted prices were raised. In any terms it was a brutal and naked display of strength. The appearance of negotiation provided a flimsy cover for a situation in which the OPEC members were virtually able to dictate unilaterally changes in contractual agreements – in spirit, if not in law, flagrantly in violation of any internationally agreed code of behavior governing contractual relationships. "The oil companies have had it," a very senior executive of one of the US majors wearily said.

At the time of this writing, the OPEC governments are girding themselves for a different campaign, designed to secure a substantial measure of participation in the producing companies. The companies have had no obligation to their host governments beyond income tax, royalties, and the many costly demands in the fine print – investment in satellite industries, infrastructure, and so on. Now it is time, an OPEC resolution states, for the governments to be brought into the companies as partners.

The governments already have a substantial degree of control. Earlier battles have secured for them the right to consultation when any increase in posted prices is contemplated; they have taken back much of the land the producing companies had under the original concessions (or rather, the companies have "relinquished" concession territory). With minor perturbations, it is an accepted principle that government revenue will never drop; all the governments are keenly interested in the level of production and sometimes successfully apply pressure to have their own share of the market increased. Some economists have suggested that in a situation where governments have secured control over a section of the industry in which profits are quite anomalously high (for reasons we shall discuss) they would be better off getting out altogether.

THE BEGINNINGS

This is a whole world away from the conditions under which the four main producing companies were set up – a process that was complete by the Second World War and set the pattern of concessions which still holds today. These had a number of leading characteristics of which, for the purposes of this case, the main ones were:

1. The concessions covered the whole country. The first one, granted by the Shah of Persia to William Knox d'Arcy in 1901, gave him "a special

and exclusive privilege to search for, obtain, exploit, render suitable for trade, carry away and sell natural gas, asphalt and ozerite throughout the whole extent of the Persian Empire for a term of sixty years." The others, made between the World Wars in Iraq, Saudi Arabia and Kuwait, granted the same territorial exclusivity.

2. Payments were to the rulers of the country — in each case absolute monarchs for whom the money was treated as personal wealth — and in the form of royalties, that is a fixed sum per barrel produced.

3. Complete commercial freedom to fix prices and production levels. (Prices were fixed at levels related to US Gulf Coast prices.) Such freedom was not in question to the degree that it needed embodying explicitly in concession agreements; it was, and largely still is, the way companies expect to be able to work.

4. Special privileges for expatriate employees. This was mostly *de facto* the result of having company settlements — such as Ahmadi in Kuwait, Abadan in Iran, and Dahran in Saudi Arabia — which were isolated from the country. But outside the settlements the employees carried the power and privilege of the companies.

5. The keen political interest of the companies' "sponsor" governments. This was partly a reflection of the territorial interests of major powers. It also had a practical side, as when the British Government took a majority share in Anglo-Persian Oil (d'Arcy's company) to secure bunkering for the British navy. Hartshorn says, "The other major operating companies . . . came into being as a result of commercial initiative more or less liberally admixed with diplomatic influence. . . What eventually became the Iraq Petroleum Company in 1928 has been the subject of commercial enterprise since 1904, with concessions sought, gained and challenged by German, Britain, Italian, Dutch and American interests. After the First World War, German interests were dropped out (being eventually handed over to France in consideration for other claims on the Near East). British and American maneuvering continued. In 1928, a group of British, Dutch, French and American companies . . . signed an agreement that allowed for the creation not only of IPC (the Iraq Petroleum Company) but also of joint companies to exploit oil in a large area of the former Turkish empire." (Readers will doubtless recall that the Turkish empire had the bad luck, or bad taste, to support the losing side in the First World War.) Gulf Oil was a party to the original IPC agreement but,

when it sold out, "in order to negotiate for a concession with the Ruler of Kuwait, it found that the British Government invoked a prior agreement by the ruler not to grant a concession to any but a British company. The upshot, in 1933, was that Gulf joined with Anglo-Persian in setting up the jointly-owned Kuwait Oil Company to sign a 75-year concession from 1934..."*

6. Interlocking ownership. The political pressures of the major powers secured the presence of US, British, French, and Anglo-Dutch companies in the Middle East. The commercial interests of the oil companies dictated a pattern of joint ownership of the producing companies by the small group of the oil majors which ensured "orderly" marketing of the crude oil – that is, the introduction of these low-cost crudes into world markets without disturbing a structure of prices based on US Gulf Coast prices.

The relationship was, not to put too fine a point on it, colonial. With the backing of their (very powerful) governments, the companies were able to act with colonialist freedom in the producing countries. Given the low costs of the crude oil – still in the range 5¢ to 25¢ per barrel compared with US costs of up to $3 a barrel – and the high prices maintained by a dominating coalition of the seven majors (Jersey Standard, California Standard, Gulf, Mobil, Texaco, Shell, and Anglo-Iranian) plus Compagnie Francaise des Petroles, it was immensely profitable. Yet we have seen at the beginning of this case that the power balance has shifted in the half-century since those first concessions.

CHANGES IN POWER

Edith Penrose, in *The International Petroleum Industry*, gives four reasons for the accession of power to the producing governments:

"First and foremost was the extraordinary value to the companies of the oil discoveries outside the US in the light of the rapidly rising demand of the industrialized world . . . [partly as a result of which] the companies were willing to concede improved terms in the Middle East.

---

*Hartshorn, J.E., *Oil Companies and Governments*, Second Edition. London: Faber, 1967, p. 314.

"Secondly, the growing oil revenues led to an increasing dependence of the economies of the producing countries on them and a growing awareness in these countries . . . of the very great value of their national resource. This in itself increased the bargaining power of the countries because the great foreign enterprises came to loom larger and larger as alien 'exploiters' in the minds of vocal political minorities. Paradoxically, the greater the need of the governments to placate aggressively nationalist groups, the greater was their bargaining power, for the companies had, in the last analysis, always to keep in mind the danger to them of more aggressive groups obtaining control of the government. . .

"Thirdly, the activities of the companies and the payments they made to governments facilitated the development of these countries and with this development came the growth of political, economic and administrative expertise which progressively decreased the inequality between the governments and the companies. . . It is inconceivable today, for example, that any government would accept the argument put forward by the Anglo-Persian Oil Company in the negotiations over the revision of the d'Arcy Concession in 1933 that a 60-year concession was a 'necessary condition for the sinking of further large capital sums in the installations in Persia'. . .

"And finally, the formation of the Organization of Petroleum Exporting Countries in 1960 very much enhanced the bargaining power of the producing countries as a group. . . OPEC was formed as an immediate response to [a cut in posted prices which would have reduced government revenues] and from that time on the companies effectively lost their freedom to alter prices unilaterally. . .

"Underlying all these developments was the clearly rising competition in the world oil industry . . . [which] brought into prominence the relationship between increased revenues for the producing governments and the rate of supply of crude oil . . . no longer would the governments be willing to view their problem as the relatively simple one of bargaining with the companies for an increased share of whatever profits the companies had decided should be attributed to crude oil."*

_____
*Penrose, Edith T., *The International Petroleum Industry*. London: George Allen and Unwin, 1968, pp. 198-200.

But before this could happen, a number of other changes took place: the introduction of an income tax to boost the old royalty income; the relinquishment of concession territories; the arrival of companies from outside the charmed circle of the majors; the development of untraditional concession terms; a number of unilateral actions, political in origin and varying in success. As with the processes of social change described earlier, these were all to a large degree linked; no one of them could be said to lead.

1. Taxes and Prices

The first change was the introduction of income tax as a basis of payment supplementing royalties. Toward the end of the 1940's the growing nationalism of the host governments was forcing companies to look for ways of increasing revenues; IPC agreed to higher royalties in Iraq, and Anglo-Iranian was involved in a long and complex negotiation with the Iranian government to the same end. But in 1950 the American shareholders in Aramco — California Standard, Jersey Standard, Texaco, and Mobil — stepped outside the existing framework with an offer of a 50-50 profits split, an arrangement some of them had experienced in Venezuela. It was simple, it seemed to be fair, and it met the political needs of the moment. Above all it was costless, since — by agreement with the US Treasury — the tax could be set against US liabilities as a credit. Before long it became the standard form of tax in the four major concessions. The result was to make it attractive for oil companies to generate almost all of the profit on the integrated operation at the producing end.

The new tax set a trap for the companies, although it was not sprung for ten years. Calculated from posted prices, it gave the governments an interest in maintaining these levels. Posted prices were artificial from the beginning; by far the greatest part of the oil was traded within the integrated activities of the companies at paper-transfer prices. However, as surpluses of oil developed in the middle and late 1950's, the companies offered to outside buyers discounts which had the effect — posted prices remaining the same — of increasing the governments' tax take as a proportion of realized prices. Attempts were made to reduce postings to keep up: Penrose points out that tax revenues in the Middle East rose by 13.7 percent compared with a 22 percent rise in production between 1959 and 1961, a difference largely attributable to reductions in posted prices.

The oil countries banded together in OPEC in 1960 with the specific objective of restoring prices to their 1958 levels. They did not succeed in this (although they forced the companies to restore the most recent price cut) but they made it impossible for companies ever again to change prices downward without consultation. This effectively froze the greatest part of the profits on the companies' integrated operations at the production stage. That is, huge paper profits are generated in the producing countries simply to be taxed — with dire effects on the financial realism of the companies' other operations, the illusions of the producing governments, and the continuing desire of other companies to get on the gravy train.

2. *"Legislate, Don't Negotiate"*

The first direct test of strength between companies and governments came with the nationalization of Anglo-Iranian Oil in 1951. Relations had worsened through the period of discussion over revenues. The company, straddling the country's most precious natural resource, its employees living high in the settlement at Abadan, had become the hated symbol of foreign exploitation. Prime Minister Mossadeq, weeping and fainting, whipped the Iranian Majlis (parliament) into a frenzy of nationalist fervor and the company concessions, plant, and refinery were made government property. But this served no real effect. Anglo-Iranian could turn to production in Iraq and to Kuwait for supplies; no buyers could be found for the oil, with Anglo-Iranian lurking around waiting to pounce with the full weight of international law. After the fall of the Mossadeq government in 1953, the affair was resolved with the formation of the Consortium — comprised of major oil companies but with Anglo-Iranian (by then British Petroleum) still as the dominating partner — to produce and sell the oil.

The failure of Iranian nationalization was not forgotten by the Middle East governments through the nationalist movements that were to follow. Further attempts to gain ground at the expense of the companies were made more judiciously and with an appearance of negotiation; the governments were to discover that they had plenty of power in reserve without contravening international law.

The next major move was made by General Qasim, who had overthrown Iraq's royal regime in 1958. In 1961 he passed "Law 80" which expropriated all but one-half percent of IPC's concession territory, leaving the producing fields in the hands of the company. Various attempts were made to come to a working arrangement; joint development was proposed, but nothing was politically acceptable. No government could make an agreement with the company without delivering itself to its political enemies; direct action would invite legal reprisals. For a combination of reasons – concerned more with the unsettled politics of Iraq than with the companies' strength – the effect of Qasim's move has been to hold back development of the country's industry.

Far more significant was the move by the Libyan government in 1965 to change the country's oil laws. (Although not in the Middle East, Libya is included in this discussion because it has played a leading part in the process of change.) A late entrant, Libya offered to oil companies in 1954 concessions that were substantially more generous than the Middle-East concessions, by then of proven value; they also offered concessions in blocks that were small by Middle-East standards. Independents – such as Marathon, Amerada, Continental, Occidental, and Bunker Hunt – who had been excluded from the Middle East by the pattern of interlocking ownership in the producing companies eagerly took the opportunity and found oil, adding greatly to the pressure on prices through their vigorous marketing efforts. By 1965 the Libyan government was ready to move from its early generosity to conditions more like those prevailing in OPEC countries. (Here they were actively encouraged by the majors among their concessionaires who preferred the higher costs of OPEC terms to the continuing disruption of their more important business elsewhere.) The Libyan government presented its companies with an ultimatum: either they would voluntarily accept the new terms or worse things would befall them: exports by recalcitrant companies would be stopped; no further concessions would be offered; certain tax claims were threatened. By the end of January, 1966, all the 24 companies in Libya – of which only six held out to the bitter end – had capitulated. Without having to resort to any sort of direct political action and risk legal reprisals, the Libyan government had demonstrated that the producer governments could take action to vary the terms of the contracts virtually with impunity. The lesson of "Legislate, don't negotiate" was well learned by the time of the events which opened this case.

3. Changing Concession Terms

Another important change over the period was in the form taken by the new concessions being allowed. In 1957 and 1958 Iran granted offshore concessions to foreign companies on a basis not only of 50-50 profit split but of half-ownership with the National Iranian Oil Company. In 1958

Saudi Arabia and Kuwait granted a concession in their jointly controlled Neutral Zone (disputed territory between the countries) to a Japanese company on conditions which included a higher tax, guarantees of investment in refineries, and an option to buy into the operating company, the Japanese Arabian Oil Company. Shell was the first oil major to take an out-of-line concession, for land offshore Kuwait, in 1961. In 1966 a new twist was introduced into this process of experiment with different terms when the French state company, ERAP, made a deal with NIOC to act as contractor — that is, not a concession-holder at all. ERAP agreed to bear all the costs of exploration simply for the right to buy any resulting crude from NIOC. The Iraq government made similar deals with companies in 1968-69 over the land taken from IPC under Law 80.

These deals are not significant in a quantitative sense, since they cover land which is by definition not a prime prospect. By a wide margin the greatest part of the oil produced in the Middle East is covered by old-style concessions. However, the old concessions will be increasingly eaten into by the relinquishment provisions "voluntarily" agreed upon between companies and their governments. These require concession-holders to give up a portion of their land on some agreed schedule for the governments to let off to other — presumably more actively interested — companies. Over time, this process will have a significant effect on the concession map and thus on the dominating power of the original producing companies in their countries.

Some of the companies are now prepared to admit that they welcome the presence of others. To be the only "foreign exploiter" in a country can be a grievous burden, requiring much expensive public relations in the form of schools, roads, hospitals, refineries, and agricultural projects. But for the most part the producing companies are preparing to hold onto their source of power (in oil industry terms) and profit for as long as it continues to be that.

4. Strategic Delay

To an outside observer, it seems clear that the landscape has changed so completely as to require substantial and voluntary changes in the stance and operations of the companies. Yet of the four major jointly held producing companies which we have discussed, only Aramco has been consistently prepared to offer its government in Saudi Arabia more than the government might have demanded. In all substantial issues the other companies have almost invariably given late and reluctant agreement to the progressively escalating demands of their host governments. There are two broad reasons for this slowness: a good deal of inertia is present in the existing ways of doing things, and the best strategy for the companies may seem to lie in delaying the inevitable as long as possible.

It has taken a long time for the companies to realize that the power which once rested in the possession of crude has gone. In the early days of the industry's development, access to crude was the main source of power in the industry. For example, British Petroleum (then Anglo-Iranian) was accepted as one of the majors only because of its enormous reserves; in terms such as downstream investment and access to markets it was almost nonexistent. It is hard for companies which have grown up in these conditions to make the abrupt switch to an acceptance of new conditions when that switch implies that the weapon in the hand has become useless. Also, the companies' management — particularly the senior management — had acquired experience in overseas operations under neocolonial conditions. And this is hard to lose, no matter how conscious the effort to adjust to new conditions. A visitor to Ahmadi in Kuwait will be impressed even today by the success with which the employees of Kuwait Oil have created a style of life that owes little to the country in which they live; Dahran, in Saudi Arabia, could be a Los Angeles suburb (except that the booze has to be homemade). This is not a particularly blameworthy fact; there was little enough there to start with. But it does quite sharply identify the company as an alien presence.

Furthermore, the power is *seen* to be elsewhere. It is only relatively recently that the local manager of Kuwait Oil has moved to Kuwait City. Even now the head offices of Kuwait Oil, IPC, and the Iranian Consortium are in London. There are good reasons for this in the shareholding companies' terms, but again it is a corroboration of the foreignness of these companies that the main decisions concerning their activities are made in another country. Even Aramco, which has always centered itself in Saudi Arabia with all the officers of the company living on the spot, is subject to tight control by its shareholders from New York.

These details reflect more than mere inertia; they reflect the priorities of the shareholding companies, each of which runs a gigantic, integrated, international business wherein the producing interests are a crucially important part — but *only* a part — of the complex whole. The chairman of one of the majors once said that the end of the companies' place in the Middle East was inevitable, ". . . the best we can hope for is to delay it."

In fact, he may have been too gloomy. The producing governments have realized the immense value of the companies' downstream investments and access to markets; it may not serve their interests at all to sever connections completely and deal at arms' length as part of a group of jostling sellers. The art of dealing with the oil companies, as an expert once said, is that of "squeezing them without actually strangling them to death." A dead milch cow is of no use to anybody.

The last word should be left to Penrose. The organization of the international oil companies was the outcome, she says,

". . . of the competition of big capitalist oligopolies, with their roots in the free-for-all attitudes of the nineteenth century and very much oriented toward the requirements of the industrialized West. After the Second World War came the so-called 'emergence' of large numbers of countries in Asia and Africa, independent . . . growing stronger in their political bargaining power, acquiring an increasing indigenous supply of knowledgeable civil servants and politicians, and imbued with a strong and somewhat touchy nationalism and spirit of independence . . . the changed position of the underdeveloped countries . . . brought about significant changes in the environment in which the oil companies operated. . . The companies were in many respects extremely slow to adjust to the new environment, on occasion at serious cost to themselves. At times, however, emotionally charged antagonism and internal politics in their host countries made serious negotiation almost impossible, leaving the companies very little room for manoeuvre. But it is not surprising that they were on the defensive, and that they should fight rearguard actions to delay changes adverse to their own interests. . . The deeper root of the problem is simply that international firms, including the oil companies, have not yet found a way of operating in the modern world which would make them generally acceptable as truly international institutions. The officials of most international firms may not as yet even attempt an international outlook, and would consider any suggestion that they might do so to be inconsistent with their national allegiance. . . But in other, more far-seeing firms (also to be found in the oil industry), officials . . . are acutely aware that in the long run the international acceptability of world-wide enterprise will depend on how successfully [these problems] are solved."*

---

*Ibid., pp. 262-263.

CONCLUSIONS

The case of the petroleum industry in the Middle East is one of a defensive response to changes in the organizations' political environment. Change there has been and plenty of it, but in contrast to the Allied Minories case there have been few attempts to *anticipate* the directions of change with appropriate changes in the organizations' internal and external relationships. Inasmuch as this was a conscious decision, it was based in a negative assessment of the companies' long-term prospects as alien presences, yet responsible for production of their host countries' only source of indigenous wealth. Short-term profit maximization may have seemed the only sustainable policy. But this in turn required another assumption: that other changes were not possible. It was almost certainly correct to conclude that the companies had no place in the Middle East in their historical form; it was not so obvious that some other relationships might have secured their presence. In fact, with the recent (1972) negotiations over OPEC countries' taking majority shareholdings in the producing companies, such institutional changes are being proposed — by the governments.

There are a number of reasons why the oil companies should have taken this path. In all of them the comparison with the Allied Minories' case is instructive, if only because so far-fetched.

First, the political nature of the changes in the companies' environment made it difficult for managers to respond to them at all, let alone intelligently. Changes in the Allied Minories environment fell (initially anyway) into that rational-economic region which managers have learned by training and experience to regard as the main legitimate focus of their attention. The political changes in the Middle East fell into "blind ground" where managers, used to the rules of operating in the stable political environments of other times and other countries, did not see them as a source of energy for organizational change. They were observed as something to be resisted, perhaps, but not to be imported into the organization.

Second, the magnitude of the changes taking place gave them more the appearance of violent revolution than of organic change, to which adaptation might have been more obviously possible. The original concession agreements embodied the political realities of 50 years ago, and they were perpetrated in the companies' contemporary values and culture. This was analogous to the Allied Minories situation. The distance traveled between the relationships embodied in the agreements under which

Kuwait Oil, Iraq Petroleum, and the other producing companies were set up and the more-than-equal relationship demanded by nationalistic governments is greater than, but of the same magnitude as, that traveled between the authoritarian "right to manage" accepted as proper by industry in the 1930's and more participative styles of management. The transition had some of the same power to outrage an almost moral sense of what was fitting.

But — and this is the third point — Allied Minories was forced to come to terms with changes in its *home* environment which could, unless accommodated within the organization, threaten its long-term survival. With the exception of British Petroleum and to a lesser extent of the other European companies, the Middle-East interests of the oil companies were, however profitable, peripheral to their main interests — particularly to the self-contained domestic interests of the dominant US companies. When decisions were being made in London and New York, it was probably easier not to allow the political factors their true inconvenient weight.

Finally, the structure of the producing companies' shareholding and the terms under which they had been set up made any except minimal change very difficult. The shareholding companies had widely divergent needs; only those policies which were acceptable to them collectively were feasible. The more conventional unitary organization of Allied Minories made adaptation possible, once the need for it was perceived. There were many individuals in the oil companies, deeply versed in Middle-East politics, who saw what was likely to happen decades before it did, but they were powerless to change policies until it was too late.

Even if the companies had been prepared to change, it is hard to see how the massive shift in the balance of power between companies and governments could have been accommodated except through changes so drastic as to modify substantially their status as private companies. The main shift arose from the growing awareness in Middle-East countries of national identities and the development of political means for expressing them. The oil companies would have had to be far more sensitive and self-sacrificing than companies commonly are to have voluntarily accommodated national aspirations in their decisions. However, some limited actions were possible.

Specifically, the producing companies were politically exposed in the narrow base of their shareholding — seven companies in control of the two-thirds of the free world's oil reserves which comprised almost the entire national wealth of Kuwait, Saudi Arabia, Iraq, and Iran. They were also exposed in their all-too-obvious foreignness and separation from the national interests of their host countries. It is quite likely that no actions could avert the inevitable end of their power as principals in the production of Middle-East oil, also that judgments made in retrospect are worse than useless. Nonetheless, it would have been prudent, to say the least, for the oil companies who were the shareholders in producing companies to have brought in other shareholders, particularly nationals of such major consuming countries as West Germany and Japan. The mode of operation – with the structure of head offices in London and New York, company towns and expatriate managers – was calculated to focus xenophobic feelings. Such changes in direction could have been based on foreseeable developments after World War II and indeed were recommended, but ignored.

Instead the companies decided, whether consciously or not, on a policy of late and reluctant submission to increasing political pressure. The prophecy – that "the end is inevitable: the best we can hope for is to delay it". – was thereby confirmed. Ironically, if the companies survive as a presence in the Middle East, it will only be through the strenuous efforts of the host governments.

SUMMARY

When a small number of large oil companies first obtained concessions in the Middle East from 1908 onward, they had positions of considerable power. As rich companies backed up by powerful governments (American and British), they dominated the unsophisticated countries of the Persian Gulf, many of which were ruled by individuals of whom they were the personal property. A series of small shifts in the balance has over the years completely reversed the situation. The companies are now largely powerless to make many of the important decisions affecting operations within the countries and even outside them, as in the case of posted prices for crude oil.

These shifts have taken place in response to changes in the political and commercial environment. Most important of all, the small countries discovered a sense of national identity and developed the means for expressing it politically. They also formed a cartel to oppose the unanimity of the companies with a united front and with time they acquired expertise in the industry to match the large companies' own. Internationally, the companies were enfeebled in their response by the fact that the tide of opinion was turning against any form of colonialism. Even if support had been forthcoming from their governments, it would not have been possible to use it. In addition to this they were the victims of their own strength as multinationals: tax concessions had made it attractive for them to so arrange their affairs that most of the profit on the integrated operations (production, transportation, refining, and distribution) was generated at the producing end, which delivered it to the governments as a suitable subject for taxation.

In this changing situation the companies have had to adjust their ideas about their position in the host countries; they have changed recruitment policy to attract locals into management; they have broken down the often exclusive communities in which expatriates lived; they have become more sensitive to the effects of their policies on local feeling. The net result has been to hand over power to a degree where their presence may be threatened.

8
BREACHING THE ORGANIZATION

The rest of the book will be concerned with the more detailed ways in which social change will manifest itself inside the organizations. I have divided the discussion into two main parts (Chapters 8 through 10, and Chapters 11 through 14) as an admittedly arbitrary division in the sources of pressures for change inside the corporation. The categories are not intended to be exclusive; as we have seen, change-processes are interdependent. The two groups are:

1. Forces for change that are felt from outside the company. Here we find two subgroups both of which focus questions about the role of the corporation in society. In time they will lead to a redefinition of that role.

a) Popular pressures. These can act directly (as with the consumer movement on issues such as corporate social responsibility) or through the agency of politics (as with pollution, which after years in the wilderness was taken up by President Nixon). The most important models of nonpolitical pressure for the near future are the consumer and conservationist movements, which are both likely to become key factors in company calculations.

b) Government pressures. There are the political and executive responses of government institutions either to popular pressure (as in the car safety and pollution issues) or more or less spontaneously to the presence of social and political problems (as with antitrust or welfare issues). Action takes the form of new laws or of measures within the framework of existing ones.

2. Forces for change that manifest themselves inside the company.

a) Upward pressures, arising from the needs and demands of the members. These include the characteristic trade-union demands for more money and better working conditions. The change that results is to a large degree enforced.

b) Downward pressures, originating within management or in some expert resource at management level. These pressures characteristically derive from new thinking about workplace relationships (as in Organization-Development activities) and often go far ahead of anything proposed by unions. The changes are offered voluntarily, since they are designed to meet needs that have not been articulated or may not yet have arisen.

This split leaves out much that is germane to the central issue of the book: changes in the social structure of organizations. Most particularly, the forces of technological and economic change act in direct opposition to the move toward a voluntary society. These are the integrating forces generated within a competitive, profit-seeking capitalist economy; they work by eliminating the slack within and between systems (systems slack is equivalent to forgone profit); and they tend to knit systems together into larger units and greater interdependency. This mode of change has been dominant in the Western industrialized world in recent history. The disintegrative move towards a voluntary society has been made possible by, and is partly in reaction against, these economic processes. I have not discussed them more fully because they are a constant factor, an integral property of the systems – and we are interested in new directions of change.

However, a new feature of the economic mode of change is the internationalization of markets and the companies trading in them. In the same way and for much the same reason that the corporation has grown, countries have grouped together to form trading blocks like the European common market. Economies of scale are as important to governments seeking to provide a market base for internationally viable industries as they are to companies seeking to beat competitors' costs. The companies have in many ways anticipated these changes, for they have been growing in size and some of them have extended their operations abroad since before the turn of the century. It was inevitable that corporations would evolve toward a more international view of their business, depending on the industry, as their growing size strained against the limitations of a purely domestic view. And technological developments in transportation, communications, and data processing have provided the means for integrating the activities of ever-larger units. The resulting internationalization of industry may be new, but the process which has engendered it is a property of the capitalist system. Thus the move toward internationalism is the logical extension of the move toward larger companies and markets that preceded it on a domestic level.

The products of economic change provide the basis for the most intense external attacks on the company. Popular movements direct their charge at the big companies, standardized products, design that concentrates only on features to which the markets will respond, the externalities of production (pollution, noise, squalor), the accelerating depletion of resources, and the domination and manipulation of the consumer. And this popular determination to take a more direct part in deciding what companies will do is likely to be an increasingly important feature of corporate life.

There have been many manifestations of campus disaffection with industry. The relative decline of engineering faculties, described in Chapter 4, partly reflects this. A more obvious sign is the frequency of attacks on companies seen to be engaged in "dirty" war industries (for example, Dow Chemicals making napalm for use in Vietnam) or doing business with "dirty" political regimes (as in the case of Chase Manhattan and Polaroid in South Africa). It would be impossible to separate such campus issues from the forces they tap. The issues are real enough, but the rapidity with which they change suggests that there is more than just an element of fashion in them; as does the fact that they move on restlessly from one vital injustice to another with no action beyond protest. However ephemeral, these campaigns can be intense: bombs in company offices and bricks through bank windows are intense protests, if limited in scope. And the intensity probably reflects the latent emotional energies which the issues, in not very mysterious ways, tap.

Such pressures cannot be satisfactorily separated from the second group of external popular pressures: movements for corporate social responsibility in matters like product design, pollution, conservation, and consumer protection. But both in their manifestations and in their effects, they are different. Readers are probably familiar with "Campaign GM," the attempt in Spring, 1970, by a group of young Naderite lawyers to enforce upon the Board of General Motors a more explicit commitment to a social role for the company. They were pressing for a commitment to safe, pollution-free automobiles; to a policy of hiring and educating blacks; and to Board representation for consumer and black interests. They were, of course, unsuccessful. However, they caused the GM Board much effort to refute the charges, and the company is certainly not the same since it has been forced to recognize explicit social obligations that extend far beyond its shareholders. One year after that campaign, a similar protest was staged in Britain against the policies in South Africa of Barclay's DCO bank. DCO has a branch network in South Africa; more heinous, it was peripherally involved in the financing of the Cabora Bassa Dam, in Mozambique. Statements were issued by the bank shortly thereafter about racial equality of pay in DCO's South African offices. The issues would have been familiar on the campus; the method of pursuing them was rooted more deeply in the methods of Ralph Nader and the consumer movement which preceded his historic attack on auto design, *Unsafe at Any Speed.*

It seems quite certain that campaigns on the consumerist model are going to generate the most powerful external influences for change in the corporation. They are a manifestation of shifts that are taking place in the balance between underlying systems in society. These are the problems generated by the huge size and power and the freedom from control of the corporations, and by the inadequacy of the market to allocate resources for the provision of social goods. As we shall see later in this chapter, moral condemnation of the corporations is beside the point; it is the system in which they operate that has created them. But the problems are there and must be dealt with. Furthermore, people are now willing to question the basic assumptions of our economic system. While accepting the usefulness of profit as a measure of some sorts of efficiency, they question whether it is enough as a measure of all actions. A growing number are questioning the value placed on economic growth. Most fundamentally, they question the absolute right to the use of property when it involves a social cost and, as we discussed in Chapter 2, the use of property has become increasingly contingent on social approval. The Government has traditionally had the function of representing the public interest, and with legislation (described in more detail in Chapter 9) it has done so. But these powers are being supplemented by consumerist and environmentalist groups which represent the beginnings of some more pervasive mechanism for making companies publicly accountable for their actions.

Pressures from these movements are felt in two ways:

1. Directly, by attacking the companies head-on; calling into question an often carefully built image of competence and professionalism; sometimes threatening actual damage to property (which is, curiously enough, a less effective means of applying pressure because it is illegal and therefore easily isolated).

2. Indirectly, by creating political issues that may attract the attention of politicians and end up as legislation. This has occurred with measures for car safety and against pollution.

The pressures have been successful because conditions have been right for this success. Some of these conditions are:

- Prosperity and a sufficient independence from the reward system that comes from it.

- Changing assumptions about the rights of property.

- Increased public awareness of the problems associated with economic growth.

- The more questioning frame of mind that comes from education and more diverse sources of information, in particular television.

- The radicalizing effect of a few major issues, such as Vietnam.

Let us look at three issues which contain some of the features we have discussed.

1. Autos

No industry better exemplifies the mixed curses and blessings of modern industrial society than motors. On the credit side, it is an enormously important part of the economy, generating jobs and wealth in the most advanced and efficient assembly operation in industry, the source of many innovations. It makes a product which grants independence and freedom of movement to industrial man.

On the debit side, the critics accuse the industry of:

- wasteful misuse of resources in providing transport surplus

- working conditions among the worst in industry
- generation through admass manipulation of an unreal "need" for surplus
- design that concentrates not on function but on salable image, resulting in products that are dangerous and dirty
- ill-effects on environment (particularly cities) of too many cars

We can see in even so sketchy a list some fundamental criticisms of the system that produces the motor company and cars. What the companies are set up to do, they do well. They exist to sell more cars, produced at lower costs, for higher prices than their competitors. They have therefore developed organizations that are miracles of engineering and administrative efficiency. And their efforts are devoted toward gaining ground in the market. Neither freedom from pollution nor the presence of safety features are selling points; the purchaser will not pay more for these social goods when he is offered the performance he wants at a lower price. Display, power, sexiness — these are selling points. Cars are therefore too numerous, sexy, overpowered, flashy, unsafe, and dirty.

We do not need a conspiracy to explain this fact. We need look no further than the dynamics of the market itself. The companies no less than their products are the distorted yet logically inevitable result of the reward system of free enterprise. The motor companies are far from the cunning, controlled manipulators of the Galbraithian myth; if they act antisocially, it is through stupidity rather than malice. The lack of balance in the product is the result of an interaction among engineering requirements, people's needs, and the strengths and limitations of promotional techniques. The hugely swollen engineering, styling, and marketing departments of a company like General Motors tell us as much about the company's purpose, needs for survival, and the demands of its environment as the teeth of a shark or the ears of a rabbit tell us about theirs.

2. Pollution

The emission of pollution is one of the ways in which industries reduce costs. It is antisocial when it affects the living environment; it is wrong (that is, immoral) when it irreversibly degrades the environment. However, there is a danger that the issue of pollution is being turned into a universal moral imperative: Thou Shall Not Pollute. Yet it is clear that almost all human activities pollute the environment, that they always have, and that far from being worse than ever before, the situation is in some ways improving. In Europe, where land is scarce and the permissible burden of pollution necessarily lower, powers have been taken by governments for more than a century over the use of land and the emission of pollution. Yet there is a movement against pollution which sees, as the only alternative, courses of action which would be politically unfeasible.

It is the very intensity of the public reaction that gives a clue to its origin. It seems clear, since the intensity far exceeds the realities of the situation, that this is one of the issues that taps into deeply hidden sources of emotional energy. In particular, the reaction draws energy from a quite reasonable fear of "Them," the deaf, impervious giants that dictate the details of our lives, stunt us in their employment, and now, it seems, want to poison us and the world. Many of the ecology lobby's prescriptions are more easily understood if they are seen as a direct attack on industry and the competitive world we have inherited.

This is not to suggest that the problem does not exist; only that it is susceptible to more rational analysis than it is receiving, and that the irrationality is a clue to the real dynamics of the movement. The propensity of modern industry to pollute is a direct product – almost a property – of the free market and the pressure within it to reduce costs. The solution to the problem is not to be found in making moral judgments about the polluters, any more than about manufacturers of unsafe and dirty cars. The answer lies in legislation that imposes on the system the costs of dealing with its byproducts, further limiting the "freedom" of the market. For it is *society* that has polluted the environment through its consumption and the effect of the price mechanism on costs. The companies are society's agents, and it is society that will have to bear the cost.

3. Apartheid

At the beginning of 1971, Polaroid Corporation advertised in all major US newspapers to announce intentions toward its business activities in South Africa. The company announced a program of training and upgrading black employees and the gift of part of its profits to encourage African education. The announcement followed a visit to South Africa by a Polaroid team which examined their operations there in response to a program of protests and pressure on the company to withdraw altogether from South Africa. Many companies have been under such pressure, but the reason why Polaroid was selected in particular was that it sells the equipment for making identification cards, the symbol of police oppression. The British bank, Barclay's DCO, came under similar pressure at shareholders' meetings later in 1971 for its involvement in South Africa and, more specifically, its involvement in the financing of the Cabora Bassa Dam in Mozambique. It, too, made announcements shortly thereafter about changes in working conditions for black and colored workers.

Such campaigns have widened the range of questions raised by the corporate responsibility issue. It has even been suggested in the *Harvard Business Review* that investment in companies engaged with "immoral" regimes should be prohibited by law. (I cannot help wondering which governments could possibly be found moral.) The idea that a company should regard itself as an instrument for doing good and politically influencing people is arresting. It is one thing to call a company to account for the antisocial effects of its operations or products. It is quite an extension of the principle to enlist its support in a fight in which neither the enlister nor the company is involved.

These three issues cover the spectrum of popular external pressures I have described. Car safety has moved into the field of a solid consumerist cause: calling the companies to account for their stewardship of the public good and applying pressure, eventually through political means, to enforce standards which the operations of the market would not provide unaided. Pollution is fundamentally the same sort of issue, following the same lines but with the extra emotional energy that comes from tapping into some very deep-seated and partly irrational fears. This feature has made it more of a political issue. The antiapartheid campaign is a sideshoot of the US domestic preoccupations with racial discrimination. But it is a more purely political issue, resting on moral indignation against an unpleasant regime. What is revealing – and points to its probably ephemeral nature – is that South Africa is not the only, nor probably the most, unpleasant regime; but it is a safer object of hate than similar regimes closer to home.

The pressures that arise from these issues – and from the broader shifts that underly them – do not fall into easily separable categories. The issues are the products of complex interactions of relatively innocent and limited decisions; the pressures they give rise to have the same mixed parentage. Thus the demand for newsprint from the burgeoning British newspaper industry one-half century ago caused the deforestation of large tracts of Canada. The caribou died for want of their staple diet of moss. Eskimos died for want of caribou. No one willed the death of the Eskimos, nor would it have been obviously necessary thirty years before to prevent the newspaper industry from increasing their papers' circulation in order to prevent the final tragedy.

Such complex interactions are a feature of modern life. If they show anything, they show that in the increasingly turbulent and interactive environment of organizations today, categories and distinctions are being eliminated.

The three issues which we have outlined contain the following pointers for companies looking into the future. The order in which they are listed is arbitrary since no one of them predominates, and indeed they are likely to interact in ways that make it difficult to separate their effects.

1. Inadequacies of the market that will become increasingly apparent as the continuing improvement of technological, financial, and administrative techniques gives business organizations the wherewithal to become better at doing less — as in the design of motor cars.

2. Relaxation in traditional constraints on individual behavior.

3. Growing awareness of individual needs (partly fostered by television, partly the product of leisure, partly of education).

4. A more discriminating and demanding environment in which the freedom of companies to run their affairs without interference will increasingly be challenged.

5. The creation of more issues through direct action by consumer groups and other independent bodies, and a willingness to make a noise until something happens.

6. Government intervention to secure the supply of social goods — set within a framework of increasing government intervention in industrial affairs in the interests of economic management.

In Chapter 9, I shall examine the government's power to affect the workings of industry, and for what ends. And in Chapter 10, I shall discuss the effects of such external pressures, in particular on the shifting definition of the role of companies in society.

SUMMARY

This chapter starts with a sketch of the scheme for the remainder of the book. It proceeds to an analysis of the pressure for change within organizations that originates in popular movements, particularly consumerism.

Direct action by groups of activists to change aspects of corporate policy provides a significant new force for change within organizations. In sum, such pressures represent a unique device through which corporations can be made accountable for the social consequences of their actions. The result will be a greater corporate sensitivity toward developing public concerns. We have seen increasing sensitivity to a number of highly visible and often politically based issues such as involvement in war industries. But most significant in the long term will be the development of consumer movements that judge companies in areas of decision making — product design and safety, plant location and operation — which have formerly been the sacred prerogative of those companies. Through public examination of the underlying assumptions as well as the practical results of such decisions, there is being effected a redefinition of the role of corporations in society.

9
GOVERNMENT LIMITATION

Industry's area of free movement is shrinking all the time. As with the wild animals of the world, cultivation is destroying its natural feeding grounds, cutting the migration paths, and forcing companies into more remote valleys. Governments are paving over the lush pastures of the free market with a mosaic of laws which, some say, stifle free enterprise. Others believe such laws make industry answer the needs of society. Both statements are true, and together they illustrate the paradox of all government in a free society. Complete individual freedom is impossible within the framework of constraints that makes society possible; corporations are subject to constraints – different ones – no less than individuals. It is only because we have inherited the dogma of the free market from the early days of industrial development that this fact seems at all remarkable.

Government moves against pollution, or the imposition of safety standards for auto design, are unquestionably restrictions on the freedom of the companies affected. In the first case they impose heavy costs for the treatment of effluents; in the second, the standards inhibit the companies' freedom to design autos with maximum market appeal at minimum cost. But because uniformly applied, they result in common increases of costs which can be recovered from the market. This is just and fair, since it is the consumers who have imposed the cost in the first place. The process is inefficient inasmuch as the abuse has to reach crisis level before there is the possibility of action, but it is hard to think of another workable process, short of a centrally directed economy.

The political response to the problems of auto design and pollution is only the latest in a sequence of government actions to combat abuses arising from the unfettered operations of the free market. The market, and the price mechanism through which it operates, is highly efficient, powerful, and flexible — but only for one thing: the allocation of resources for the provision of market goods. By definition it cannot allocate resources for the provision of nonmarket goods, such as safe autos, clean air, and (some time back) unadulterated food. Nor does it contain the means to correct abuses of the system itself: the use of economic power to distort the market, as with cartels, or to exploit the economically underprivileged, as with the treatment of workers in 19th-Century Britain. The government has had to intervene, since the system provides for no other action.

But the areas of intervention are changing. The changes reflect the elimination of old abuses such as the grosser excesses of nineteenth-century capitalism. They also reflect the growth of new economic distortions, such as conglomerate growth; the development of a deeper understanding of the possibilities of economic management that followed the Keynesian revolution; and a greater public sensitivity to what constitutes antisocial acts, as with the pollution and safety issues. The sequence of government interventions in the affairs of industry can be seen as a series of responses to crises in the economy, defined on shifting ground.

The development of antitrust legislation in the US demonstrates the ways in which the government responds over time to issues that change in form. The Sherman Act of 1896 was initially a populist measure to quiet public fears at the growth of such concentrations of economic power as Rockefeller's Standard Oil Trust. With the help of the more specific provisions of the Clayton Act, the great trusts were broken up. These laws gave the antitrust division of the Department of Justice powers enough to deal with abuses of commonly defined monopoly. The Celler-Kefauver Amendment of 1950 marked a change in the target, from monopoly to oligopoly and from market-sharing arrangements to the preemption of competition by acquisition. The 1950's and early 1960's saw considerable activity in combatting anticompetitive concentration by merger. Then came the conglomerate boom – fuelled not by industrial or market logic but by tax and accounting anomalies – and the focus shifted a little more. Each time it has shifted into the region of corporate freedom, less pushing than pulled-in by the discovery of new problems or, to put it another way, the discovery by private industry of new ways to get around the laws. Thus the ideal of a freely competitive society (which has never existed in either social or economic terms) could not long survive the new abuses of power that industrial development made possible.

This is not to suggest that the powers taken are always benevolent in application. For example, it is generally accepted that powers of regulation over statutory monopolies is inevitable. But the network of regulatory agencies that has resulted has not helped the regulated industries efficiently to serve the public interest. Indeed, obedient to the law governing such relationships, the agencies have – according to economist George Stigler – become clients of the industries they are meant to regulate.

The main accession of power in the West came with the development of a deeper understanding of the workings of the economy, first implemented in an attempt to deal with the effects of the Depression of the 1930's. The debate that has raged between monetarists and fiscalists gives us a measure of the extent of macroeconomic management in a modern state. However, governments have always raised taxes. What is more characteristic of the modern state is the extent of involvement with industry at the detailed level. This takes several forms:

• The balance of spending has swung away from the private and toward the public sector. The governments of all major industrialized countries now spend a far higher and still increasing proportion of the gross national product than ever before. This reflects a greater range of functions – welfare functions, particularly in Europe; higher defense spending; increasingly elaborate programs of investment in roads, airports, and the like. It is manifested in immensely more expensive, elaborate government administrative apparatus and armies of government employees. In sum, this shift is a massive accession of power to the government.

• The interest of government in resource planning is increasing. The planning controls common in land-scarce Europe have no real equivalent in the USA. But it is certain that the growing scarcity of land and the pressures of the conservation and antipollution lobbies will cause something of the sort to develop in the USA. In Europe the planning powers have been combined with macroeconomic considerations to provide tools for implementing regional policies. Combined with investment incentives, the government has gained powerful means for influencing industrial growth on a regional basis in order to preserve regional balance.

• National economic planning is being attempted, with varying success, in countries endeavoring to maintain balance between the resources available and some priority of national economic needs. As yet the planning has hardly passed the "jaw-boning" stage of indicative plans at different levels of formality. It is unlikely to move all the way to the powers used in the centrally planned economies of the Communist and developing countries. But all plans, however indicative, provide more tools through which industry is influenced.

• Detailed intervention in the management of crucial or problem industries is now standard. The chosen instrument in the USA is the regulatory agency. But the close connection between government departments and industry to control the huge defense and aerospace spending is probably far more influential. In Europe outright nationalization for social or economic reasons is accepted; in the USA it is present but heavily disguised.

• Governments are playing a larger part in funding research and development where the indivisibilities of technological investment put such spending beyond the reach of private companies. In the US this has taken the form of sponsored research in companies and universities; in Britain the government has set up its own laboratories.

These instruments logically fit together along a scale of increasing detail at the level of intervention. Balance of payments, growth, and employment considerations set the framework within which regional and sectoral policies can be worked out. Or they could be, if the governments so chose – which in the West they mostly do not. However, as the understanding of economic processes grows, the temptation to take a grip on particularly troublesome industries or on problems of regional balance is bound to grow too. With the increasing importance of the government as a major source of funds in the private sector, this comprises a powerful force for further integration between public and private sectors.

The last Labor Government in Britain (1965-1970) was characterized by what the Prime Minister called "purposeful intervention" in industry. A new Ministry of Technology was set up in which specialized departments were given wide powers over industries – shipbuilding, computers, and machine tools received particular attention. The ultimate weapon of intervention was devised in the Industrial Reorganization Corporation. With $360 million to draw upon, I.R.C. was given an open remit to roam through industry looking for trouble and providing ways of dealing with it. As its name suggests, the central concern of the I.R.C. was with structure, and its main function was the encouragement of mergers.

In France the officials of the *Plan Indicatif* have considerable influence in the industries for which they have particular responsibility. As in other Western countries, the influence is not exercised directly but through suasion. In the USA any formal planning procedure would probably be unacceptable to the public. However, the reports of the President's economic advisers are at least as comprehensive as anything needed for planning purposes elsewhere. President Nixon's "jaw-boning" and such incidents as President Kennedy's steel-prices row point to a sort of indicative interventionism.

The process of integrating government and industry is not asymmetrical. The power may rest with the government, but it carries reciprocal responsibilities and creates reciprocal opportunities for exercising influence. The very close relationship between industry and the Department of Defense in Washington has long been a matter of comment. At any point of contact where the government is attempting to influence industry toward a particular course of action, there exists the opportunity for a counterflow of influence. And wherever the government exercises influence, it takes on part of the responsibility for the survival of the companies. There is nothing particularly sinister about the government's voting funds to succor Lockheed, yet neither was there any necessary reason why it should come to the assistance of Tristar, a civil project. But in so doing the government has recognized an obligation to a client industry. In taking over Penn Central the government was primarily recognizing the need to maintain a social service; but it was also acknowledging an obligation to an industry in whose management it has become inextricably entangled.

This process is a quite inescapable part of modern life. Every time a government department decides to standardize on a piece of equipment – with all the benefits of rationalization, lower costs, and the rest – it knits another part of society into the seamless fabric of corporate efficiency. No part of the aircraft industry, for example, is separate from the "air system." Rules for safety, standard equipment at airports, the need for uniformity even among international airlines all set a framework within which the actions of the parts — the plane, engine, and component manufacturers; the airlines, airports, and other suppliers — are integrated.

National economies are becoming related through the need to maintain stability in international currencies. Agencies like the International Monetary Fund exercise considerable influence over the domestic policies of potential sources of instability: France and Britain have in recent years both received loans from the I.M.F. in return for promises of certain action designed to improve their balance-of-payments troubles. On the other side of the scale, the extraordinary success Japan is enjoying in export markets raises questions about permissible "freedom" in international trade. The noises coming from both the USA and the EEC, worried for vulnerable industries, suggest that rules may be devised that will limit such untrammeled power, much as the Robber Barons were subjected to limitations at the turn of the century. They were too successful for the safety of society's members. The initial response may be a reversion to piecemeal protectionism for domestic reasons, but it seems likely that this would be regularized into an extension of the rules of the General Agreement on Tariffs and Trade. Thus the integrative economic processes move to knit even national economies together.

These changes are being played out against the backdrop of increasing public awareness described in the previous chapter. Legislation on pollution originated with pressure from the environmentalist lobby. Indeed it is this capacity of popular movements to create issues with political potential that is their greatest strength. Companies would rather act with the appearance of freedom and concede what is being demanded well short of government action. But this is not always possible: even if the auto companies had wanted to introduce uniform safety features in their cars, antitrust provisions would have prevented them.

The shifts in government/industry relationships described in the second case (Oil Companies in the Middle East) combine all these features. The increasing powers taken by host governments over their producing companies are a reflection of politically dangerous pressures — mainly Arab nationalist pressures — that have built up in the people of these countries. They are a recognition of the importance of petroleum to the countries' economies and a determination to gain control over it. They are also an attempt to correct what are seen as abuses of the economic system which allows the companies so to order their affairs that the greatest part of the wealth from the petroleum goes to them rather than to the countries whose sole source of indigenous wealth it is. The result has been that the host governments have progressively limited the companies' freedom of action.

The case of Western investment in the Middle East is a somewhat extreme model of government intervention. Including a repudiation of the principles of international law, it may not provide an accurate guide to what will happen in the West. But the reasons we have cited leave little doubt that the detailed interest in industrial affairs — and the corresponding power of industry to influence government — will steadily increase. It is another of those steady social changes which over time amount to huge shifts in the power balance. With the growing popular willingness to call companies to account for their actions, these forms of external pressure comprise a significant force for change within the organization. In Chapter 10, I shall indicate some of the consequences.

SUMMARY

The history of relations between government and industry is marked by a sequence of actions which has made the government a more important partner in corporate decisions. The sequence marks a progressively more complex recognition of distortions and abuses arising from the free-market system, and the reactions of governments to correct them. Antitrust, the British Factory Acts, food and packaging laws, drug safety laws, and auto safety standards all represent a diminution of the company's freedom of action; they also mark points at which private industry has been made to answer to social needs which the market system does not recognize. The process will continue, integrating government and industry as social awareness increases. But it is not one-sided, since it gives industry power in government by the same means that government is taking power in industry.

10
REDEFINING THE CORPORATE ROLE

The popular and government pressures on corporations will lead in the long term to a redefinition of their social role. Thus they are continuing a process which has made companies increasingly responsible over the past century for the social consequences of their commercial actions. In the shorter term, however, relations with a changing environment are bound to be defensive: like all systems, corporations react in ways that are intended to maintain internal stability. And in the environment the most threatening pressures are those arising from popular movements, because they represent a source of uncertainty. The forces exerted by governments on companies are far more powerful, but paradoxically they are more easily dealt with.

The battery of instruments through which government can influence companies is awe-inspiring. As we discussed in Chapter 9, they include the power to limit availability of resources by taxation and planning restrictions; the power to make and enforce laws covering nearly every aspect of the company's operations; the power as the dominant buyer of industrial goods. But because they have evolved over long periods and are steadily applied for relatively predictable purposes, they do not constitute a threatening uncertainty in a company's environment. They constitute a set of increasingly elaborate constraints within which the company can operate by developing specialized functions to manage crucial areas of interaction. With the existence of legal and financial advisers, no company has an excuse for running across the antitrust laws or the laws on accounting and disclosure. In industries such as defense and aerospace, where the government is the main – sometimes the only – customer, the importance of these areas of interaction is sufficient to dominate management decisions.

The effect of these developments on the internal workings of organizations is seen in a quite organic evolution of new structures designed to handle the demands of this new environment. Vice presidents, and sometimes presidents, of major aerospace companies have set up shop in Washington, D.C. to manage large departments whose sole purpose is the establishment of efficient working relationships with the relevant government departments. Traditional sales efforts dwindle as the company applies its resources where the effort is needed. The same process can be observed in regulated industries, particularly utilities, where a considerable effort goes into maintaining a relationship with the agency concerned. In such ways, certain functions of industry and government are integrated – a process Professor Galbraith has described as leading to a new industrial state, and summed up in President Eisenhower's phrase, "the military-industrial complex."

Where policies are consistent the relationship is a source of stability rather than uncertainty and, as such, is desired by the organization even at a cost of reduced profitability. Moreover, it provides the means through which industry influences government, still further reducing the uncertainty in its environment.

By the opposite argument, changes in the direction of government policy are particularly threatening to companies. Such changes have provided the main source of complaint in Britain after some years of "purposive intervention" that started with the 1965 Labor administration. British company chairmen make mandatory speeches about the impossibility of working with constant interference from the government. Such speeches can usually be analyzed into two main issues – restrictions on their use of resources through taxation or planning, and uncertainty. The first is a constant feature: no one cares for taxation. But the determined, although sometimes inconsistent, efforts of the government to improve the efficiency of British industry left many companies in a state of numbed confusion. Antitrust policy was applied in ways that seemed to have little of the internal logic of, for example, US policy and left companies without the capacity to predict the government response to their actions. Greater powers over the use of land and investment were taken in the interests of a regional policy. An agency, the Industrial Reorganization Corporation, was set up to assist in the restructuring of some ancient industrial messes. Without passing judgment on these actions, the effect on the environment of industry was to increase the uncertainties which the companies had to handle. The main point is that while government pressures on the corporation are usually unwelcome, they are only threatening to the internal stability of the organization when they introduce uncertainty into its environment.

It is for this reason that I have suggested the most threatening of the external pressures on the corporation — those with greatest potential for change — are the ones described in Chapter 8. Popular pressures are unpredictable, unmanageable, and are becoming a rich source of uncertainty. Companies have reacted to minimize their effects in three interdependent ways:

1. Accepting the Radicals' Case. Managers like to be on the side of the angels, and when they are convinced of the harmfulness of some practice — or its danger to the company's future — they may act to remedy it, if they can afford to. This includes voluntary action to clean up effluents; nondiscriminatory hiring practices; training programs; changes in product design. It also includes more overtly socially aware activities such as setting up funds for the encouragement of black capitalists; the IBM factory in the black ghetto slum of Bedford-Stuyvesant or Avco's printing works in a similar area of Boston, the Polaroid mission to South Africa.

2. Public Relations. Companies wish to change their status as target and stress in publicity their most socially aware, conservationist face. Hence the advertisements which show the effort being made to clean up effluents or the involvement with local problems. The education effort made, for example, as part of college recruiting campaigns falls under this heading, although it is logically an attempt to change the environment rather than disguise (or reveal in its full glory) the company.

3. Boundary Control. This is the purpose of the offices set up in a scramble in the late 1960's when the corporation became a political target to rival the Pentagon. Their names — Community Relations, Social Affairs, and so on – are explicit enough. The offices handle social problems as they arise and advise the Board on the social consequences of its major decisions. Their function is to mediate fluctuations in the environment and minimize their influence on the internal stability of the organization.

These responses are basically defensive, designed to maintain the status quo within the company – and none the worse for that. It is an important property of all systems that they move to resist influences that threaten their internal stability; no social organization would last for long without this property which provides an element of inertia in the change process and allows changes in the organization to "track" the more rapid fluctuations in its environment. The effort to handle pressures for change takes the form of resistance, and lasts only as long as the threat from outside is seen to be real, or until the change has been assimilated. But by then the organization will have changed in ways that are not consciously contrived.

General Motors defended itself successfully against the "Campaign GM" at the beginning of 1970. But the effort was a large one, costly and exhausting to the executives of this most powerful company. Having successfully held the Naderite campaigners at bay, however, it is a fair guess that GM has itself changed in the direction they would want. The effort of resistance has produced some change; more important, never again can the managers regard themselves as immune to the wishes of the community. Any company that makes any move to meet these pressures – even pensioning off an elderly vice-president to run a token social affairs office – has taken a small step in the same direction. Advertisements designed to show a company's most socially aware face must, however cynical the motivation, change the management's view of itself. Even those companies that have put out lies about their efforts in this field – and there have been some – must be affected; they are forced to defend existing activities, but it is inconceivable that their policies to the next major investments will be unaffected.

"The Happy Hypocrite," an optimistic little fairy tale by Max Beerbohm, illustrates this behavioral approach to change very well. The hero, Lord Hell, was a particularly wicked man, adept at every vice and corruption of fashionable society. He had the misfortune, or perhaps it was good fortune, to fall in love with a virtuous girl. She could not marry him, simple soul, because his face, reflecting the life he led, was not saintly. So he had a saintly mask made and adopted matching saintly manners. In this way, he won his love, married her, and retired – still behaving in a saintly fashion — to the country. One day the mask fell by accident from his face. He was certain that he would lose his wife now that she knew the truth. But the face had grown so to resemble the mask itself that she saw no difference. They lived happily ever after.

It is, as I say, an optimistic parable. And the lesson for organization change is a subtle one: however calculating the motives behind a change in organization behavior, the effects on norms and values are incalculable.

This is the slow process by which change is introduced into the organization: a massive attack; indignant rebuttal; small resulting shifts in the underlying attitudes. It is part of the processes of natural change described earlier, and its key feature is its evolutionary unplanned nature. Over time, as we noted in Chapter 2, such small changes yield revolutions. But time is running out; the change in the social environment is increasingly rapid. And if revolutionaries demand changes *now*, corporations will have to learn to adopt a more conscious attitude to change, planning for it and not simply reacting to the demands of the environment.

The external pressures on the corporation center on its role in society — as employer, as polluter, as manufacturer of goods, as the user of scarce resources, as an important part of the strength of other systems. Without getting into the debate over the real nature of corporate motivation (growth versus profit), the corporation has traditionally been seen as a morally neutral body; inasmuch as it performs these roles, they are subsumed in the main economic purpose of the company. But it is clear that while the market is an irreplaceably efficient instrument for some purposes, it does not serve for others. Governments have reserved for themselves the right to intervene and to make rules that safeguard the public interest against the blind workings of the market.

The case of oil companies in the Middle East is a clear example of this process. The host governments did not see that the oil companies were serving their national interests. They introduced laws that secured an increasing proportion of the senior jobs for their nationals. They increased their tax "take" for the benefit of national economic development. At the time of the Arab-Israeli War, they involved the companies by banning exports of oil to countries that were thought to have been Israel's allies. In spite of the moral outrage felt and expressed by the Western oil companies, this is common enough in the West: all governments raise taxes; the US government has for some time put an embargo on trade by US companies with China. Restrictions of this sort comprise distortions of the market in the interests of social goods.

Now it is the turn of popular movements to call the companies to account for the social consequences of their commercial actions. They are doing this because technology and their great size give companies even greater power in the market, and immunity from any form of social accountability; the resulting abuses can be dangerously greater. They are also calling for social accountability because in the emergent voluntary society people are less prepared to accept as inevitable the antisocial consequences of the impersonal operations of great systems – of laws, religion, or economics. In the voluntary society people question what is happening if it does not suit them. An appeal to the sacredness of the market, or to the overriding importance in the market process of making profits, will not be accepted as a justification for the production of dangerous motor cars, say, or the despoilation of the countryside. An essential part of this change is, of course, the recognition of these phenomena as social problems. But having identified them (and the problems will shift and change, since public interest is fickle), no company can feel secure behind a position of moral neutrality or of being no more than a part of the economic system.

The question companies must ask is this: How can these issues be recognized *before* they arise, possibly to be enshrined as restrictive legislation? And when crucial issues are identified, the companies must then decide whether to move to anticipate public action or, as the oil companies have done in the Middle East, delay the inevitable end for as long (and as profitably) as possible. The parallel is a misleading one, since companies have no option to continuing in business in their home country except extinction. But the response – of least and slowest change – is characteristic of industry.

To anticipate such changes, companies must learn to scan their external environment in methodical ways, watching for the emergence of new value systems, new issues, new preoccupations that might become dominant and relevant to their business. It is possible to think of techniques that could be devised for recognizing the stage of growth of such value systems; the frequency of mention in the press would be one leading indicator. But the use of these data would not be straightforward. Simple recognition of the potential force of the antipollution campaign would be unlikely to induce a pulp company to invest in effluent treatment for an existing plant: they will probably wait for legislation. However, conclusions about the ways in which opinion is forming up for action on issues of importance to the company should be an essential input for major investment decisions.

The recruitment and training policy of companies demands even more understanding of the environment. Companies recruit and train managers for their own (and other companies') needs some years ahead. The unseemly scramble for minimally qualified black managers that followed the race troubles in the Detroit motor industry could have been avoided with some foresight. If the need to provide promotion opportunities for minority races had been recognized, the complicated job not only of training them but also of preparing the ground and changing attitudes among other managers could have been undertaken more easily and with less raw results. This is not to suggest with all the benefits of hindsight that the very major social and urban problems that produced the riots in 1969-70 could have been bypassed, but rather that the companies would have been in better shape to handle them if they had anticipated the inevitable.

Another source of new ideas will come from the growing international interactions within and among multinational companies. European hiring policies are a good deal more humane than those of the US and are an inseparable part of the gentler pace of life. American companies may have to learn how to make a less ruthless policy toward workers and managers work in answer to a demand for more humanity in the workplace; at the same time, European companies will have to curb excessive softness, which in some cases is pricing them out of world markets. This counterflow of influence has been apparent in products and technology for some time — for example, in the mostly unsuccessful attempts by GM and Ford to impose US marketing patterns on the European markets and the counterflow of European influences on auto design. Some of the most interesting experiments in workplace relations — described later — are taking place in Europe, and taking place in a framework of assumptions that pays more specific attention to the social nature of commercial activities than is current in the USA.

The debate on the social obligations of the corporation has been much more prominent in the USA than in Europe; but European companies have traditionally seen themselves as having more of a social function. The very un-American lengths to which this can be taken is well-illustrated in the true story of a British company which was the monopoly producer of a basic industrial raw material. Because of the monopoly and a sense of public responsibility, profits were held below the average rate for the company's other products. In fact, they were held so low that the company decided it could no longer afford to make the product and sent a senior manager to major customers offering to provide know-how in setting up their own plants. The manager was told unanimously that the customers had no intention of getting into that business, and had his company thought of putting their prices up? They had not, and were grateful for the tip.

A number of companies have traveled far enough down this road to draw up statements of the company objectives which include substantial social elements. Shell Refining of Britain has a statement of primary objectives that starts, unexceptionably, with the requirement "to maximize its contribution to the long-term profitability of the Shell Group." The statement continues: "The resources to which it has legal rights of privileged access are nonetheless part of the total resources of society as a whole and are, in this sense, social resources; the Company believes that they must be protected, developed and managed as such." In fact, many managers if pressed to list their objectives beyond the primary ones of return on capital or profit margins, would admit to a more complicated list of obligations to the workforce, the local community, the government of the nation, and the environment, all of which act as constraints.

This growing awareness of the manifold responsibilities of business constitutes a redefinition of the role of corporations in society which could have great significance. When a school of economists is raising its voice around the world and asking questions about the assumed value of endlessly projected economic growth, it is not surprising that considerations should be introduced into the purpose of the corporation more complicated than merely adding to that growth. Such a change of emphasis will be significant, for it raises the question of what would be the purpose of commercial organizations in nongrowth economies. The aid given on many occasions by governments to failing industries — to preserve services (as with the Penn Central), to provide jobs (as with the rescue of the Clyde shipyards in Scotland), or to create new, viable societies in poor regions (as with the Cassa di Mezzogiorno in Italy) — suggests that the answer is not simple.

But these are questions companies must ask. The environment in which they operate is changing so fast that it must be constantly monitored and checked against the company's activities. Only then will it be possible for a company to talk of planning for change.

SUMMARY

External pressures on the corporation center on the issue of its role in society. The corporation responds to these pressures in ways that seek to maintain its internal stability. Although more massive, government pressures are a lesser source of anxiety to companies than is the prospect of the popular pressures discussed in Chapter 8. Government pressures are relatively steady and predictable; indeed the closer relationships with industry are a source of stability. But the popular pressures of consumerism and environmentalism are a source of uncertainty. Companies have developed three main ways of dealing with the uncertainty: change in policy, public relations, and boundary control. But this is a reactive response to change. They must learn to scan and monitor the environment for the emergent systems which set their future, and then to anticipate the change. Such moves are leading to a redefinition of the social role of organizations.

11
SOCIAL CHANGE AND THE MANAGER:
ENFORCED CHANGE

When a company makes a major change in practice, it is hard to be entirely sure about the motivation. Altruism and expediency can be so closely mixed that no separation is possible. I am therefore a little wary of describing the changes made to meet demands that arise within the company as "enforced." For example, unions make claims for more money or, rarely, for better working conditions. When managers concede these improvements, they are to some degree enforced. But the confrontation takes place within an understood framework, and more often than not both managers and unions know very well what sort of increase is appropriate before the bargaining begins. They would not, however, have made an offer without the demand. This is the first distinction: where does the change originate? Is it reactive or proactive change?

The modes of change that will be discussed in Chapter 13 are voluntary in that they originate within management and comprise a package which may be far ahead of anything the members of the organization would demand. In the case of Allied Minories the company was faced with a situation that demanded a reform of the pay structure — for internal motivational and external commercial reasons. But it went a good deal further in setting up a pay structure and a pattern of working that attempted to tap into the untouched reservoirs of motivation in the workforce. This was a voluntary initiative of the management; it was also enforced by their expectations of the way conditions would develop. Thus to some degree all change is enforced. So to the first distinction I have made — "Where did it originate?" — I will add, "and to meet what circumstances?" That is, change can be voluntary when designed to anticipate or meet conditions that have not yet transpired.

In this chapter, we are concerned with changes that are made to meet demands arising within the membership of the company — reactive and short-term. It is the mode of "natural" change, the main way in which organizations have always changed. It is a response to crisis, the way in which the greatest part of managerial decisions arise. The crises take many forms, starting with the obvious periodic union confrontation over the renegotiation of contracts — a ritual so well understood that management is able to prepare the company and its customers by stocking up ahead of the event, with the help of the union members. At the other extreme is the series of shifts so small and so trivial that they pass without notice — the minutiae of offices and plants, in which size of room, length of lunch hour, and independent action in small things mark the shifting front of some boundary. Over time, they amount to significant changes, as in the sequence of shifts through which the relative positions of manager, foreman, and shop steward have been redefined in Britain over the past twenty years. Unpublished studies in a major chemical company showed that more than half of the works managers' time was being taken up in dealing with matters of man management. The managers' attitude to this state of affairs was that their time was being wasted; their skills and experience equipped them to handle the urgent technical problems arising in the works. The attitude was rooted in a perception of normality often formed in the managers' early days, when indeed a manager had been concerned almost entirely with technical problems. The problems of man management were left to the foreman, who also had powers to hire and fire. But with time and changes in the employment environment, the salience of problems had changed. The foreman was without power to do much more than administer and coordinate the work of his group; problems involving the workforce were handled by shop stewards — previously obscure figures — and more senior managers; the solution of technical problems was pushed into the management structure. The shift was neither right nor wrong; it had taken place in response to complex shifts in the working environment and represented, in sum, a change in the salience of problems faced by management.

The influence of the environment is crucial. In the chemical company, as in the Allied Minories case, there were marked differences which could be correlated with local conditions – the industrial history, unemployment, amount and type of competitive employers, and local political tradition. These influences manifest themselves within the company as ideas and aspirations imported from different cultures by new entrants, demands from the workers and their trade unions, or as ideas that become currency through the medium of, say, television.

NEW IDEAS

The study into the market for engineers described in Chapter 5 demonstrates some of the ways in which the aspirations of new graduates become a force for change within companies – when full employment permits. It demonstrates a shift in the balance of power in the labor market and a concurrent shift in underlying assumptions about the appropriate roles of managers and employees. The shift appears in many apparently trivial ways. But it is significant, since the power which companies have to influence their employees' behavior is a function of their power in the labor market – supported by the other value systems of society.

A young man who hoped for a job in a large company 10 or 15 years ago was also hoping for an entree to a world of secure employment and material plenty. The price demanded by the company was high. It wanted evidence of good academic performance (which incidentally gave power to the colleges to enforce their own standards). The company could also demand a neat and tidy appearance, impeccable private life, and capacity for hard work. No novitiate priest would be more closely watched for signs of a failing vocation or indicators of his usefulness to the company. Many people have written eloquently about the resulting organization man in the grey flannel, Brooks Brothers' suit: risk-averse, safe, cautious; a devoted Company man and, at his best, highly professional.

In spite of the example of the engineers, much of this is still true in the big, well-established companies that have large rewards to offer. The managers who set the tone have served their apprenticeship; campus disturbances notwithstanding, there are plenty of aggressively ambitious basketball scholars from Midwestern colleges to keep them going for some time yet. And as I suggested in Chapters 4 and 5, the values embodied in this system are confirmed and strengthened by the value systems in which the organization is embedded – still standing for the "Protestant" virtues of hard work and sober conformity. But even with that support, the value systems of the organization cannot remain in one place. Every new entrant imports something slightly different from his own environment; he may have to please his bosses, but he will never be quite like them.

This uneasy tension was much in evidence during my year as a Sloan Fellow at MIT's Sloan School. The Sloan Program comprises mainly mid-career mid-thirties middle managers from large corporations in the public and private sectors: companies in industries such as aerospace, petroleum, autos, computers, government departments, and the services. We arrived full of the habits of our working environment: sober, dedicated, ambitious men. As the year progressed, deviations from the organization norm began to appear: hair became longer, mustaches sprouted like weeds, colored shirts and (harmless) irregular habits flourished. But a visit from a senior executive in one of the Sloan Fellows' companies – a fairly frequent occurrence – would often have the effect of turning a timidly blossoming nonconformist back into a company man overnight.

New ideas are imported into areas of the company's business where the labor market for special skills gives a large measure of power to their possessors. In one large company, putting together a team for a tricky software project, a key programmer asked for, and got, two weeks unpaid leave out of every six to do social work. Yet it had been an unbreakable rule of the corporation that there would be no part-timers on the payroll, let alone ghetto-working part-timers. High technology companies, such as TRW Systems, allow their employees a large degree of freedom, particularly in research areas where creativity is vital. Even in IBM it is said that research and development workers are allowed to deviate markedly from the house style of white-shirted dark-suited conformity. US law firms that have been accustomed to taking their pick from the best law schools are finding that they can get the brightest graduates only with the promise of time off for unpaid legal work on social issues. The examples could be multiplied endlessly. For me the most revealing example was found in the central situation in Altman's film, *M*A*S*H*. The two rebels in the film were highly skilled surgeons. The fun lay in their total indifference to the rules and traditions of army life. But the sting was drawn somewhat by the fact that the army's need for their skills gave them a privileged position. Their pranks became the tolerated misbehavior of aristocrats.

New ideas are imported into the business environment by the constant growth of new companies. A new generation of millionaires comprises a body of employers with an outlook quite different from that of existing companies. The vigorous electronics and aerospace companies which have been spun off from the universities of California and the Boston area are very far from the megacorporation in style and outlook. Their owners value performance first; details of behavior count less.

More important than any of these in the change process is the new intake which goes every year into the corporations from colleges. Research has shown how hard and painful is the process by which these new entrants are socialized into the business environment. But every action has an equal and opposite reaction: the work done on changing the recent graduates has to result in a corresponding amount of work on the company. And socialization can never be complete. The new company man can never quite lose a faint perfume of his college ideals. As a consequence, the radicalism of the universities will be translated, much diluted, into the new managerial styles of ten years hence. Recent classes at the Harvard Business School have conducted polls to determine which of the companies in the market for MBA's were the most socially enlightened. If the very center of the business establishment is in a mood of doubt, change must be inevitable.

These modes of change are quite specifically American. There is some degree of disaffection on the European campuses but nothing of US proportions – a fact I attribute to the level of prosperity as much as to cultural norms. Moreover, the grip of company orthodoxy is still strong. The graduate faces fewer opportunities than his US counterpart; and it is still the tradition in Europe to commit one's self for a career in a single company. However, as we shall see in Chapter 13, it is in Europe that the most imaginative experiments are taking place in the style of management and relations with workers. But this is "top down" voluntary change.

TRADITIONAL ANTAGONISMS

Managers are more likely to pay attention to pressures for change that have the sanctions of industrial action behind them. But it is a curious fact that this power is only used in limited ways (discussed later in this chapter under "Failure of the Unions"). The ruling assumptions of modern industry are the assumptions of the wage/work bargain: specifically, that rational economic man works for money and not to obtain any deeper satisfactions. If a high degree of skill is required, if the job is physically taxing or unpleasant, a high wage will reflect the degree of inducement needed. The task, the technology, and the need to devise the best

production: these are the leading considerations. The content of the work
is secondary.

Readers are probably familiar with this line of argument, and may also
be familiar with the work of motivational theorists like Abraham Maslow
and Frederick Herzberg. Changes in working conditions that are volun-
teered by management to take account of the "wholeness" of their
workers are significant. But they are not widespread.

It is characteristic of the US industrial scene that workers move from
one employer to another (in Europe this is much less common), a practice
which results in a loss of investment in training. This can be tolerated if
the training is inexpensive, as for the unskilled work of production lines.
Where skills become more special and the cost of training increases,
however, companies are finding it sensible to create conditions of work
that are an inducement to workers to stay. It is for these reasons that a
company like Texas Instruments has devoted considerable effort to
designing more content into its jobs and working conditions. And it is
significant that these improvements are made in advance of any demands
from the unions. Texas Instruments is a nonunion company and as a
matter of policy (along with such other companies as Polaroid and IBM)
offers more than any union would demand — largely to make unionization
unattractive and partly because the management sees some things more
clearly than the unions.

However, this sort of response to the problem is exceptional. It is
more usual to respond by arranging work so that the company can live
with a high turnover of relatively unskilled people. That is, the production
process is organized to minimize the skills content.

Arguments about the importance of job content are fully explored in
the work of Herzberg and others. The important point is that in many
parts of modern industry the work is so designed that there is little
intrinsically to retain either the worker's imaginative interest or his person.
He will probably be bored; the contrast with expectations generated by a
combination of education and television may induce a feeling of
frustration. The boredom and frustration finds relief either in frequent
changes of jobs, in strikes, or in devising ingenious ways to evade his work.
Many managers with shop floor experience must know the sense of relief
in a shop when some little drama breaks into the monotony. We are
experiencing more of these dramas, and on a larger scale, as the workforce
gains power to go with a growing sense of individual independence.

The law in the US imposes a degree of discipline that limits the workers' freedom to wage war on the employers through unofficial, or wildcat, strikes. For reasons that lie deep in the history of the trade union movement, the unions in Britain are not so trammelled; thus the unofficial strike is the dominant feature of British industrial life. Germany, which has had a relatively trouble-free strike record until recently, is showing significant increases in industrial action — thought by some observers to represent a late reaction against the traditionally authoritarian policies of German management.

Companies respond in different ways to this situation depending on their technology and their willingness to live with an increasingly unruly and footloose workforce. But as they design the real skill out of the jobs, they will create worse conditions which will make it more difficult to attract high-class workers and to hold onto the ones they have. I see no way out of this diminishing spiral except to break out of it with a pattern and method of working which will restore to the worker some of the interest in his work that is the only long-term hope for stability.

FAILURE OF THE UNIONS

We might expect unions to play a leading part in these changes, since they have been largely instrumental in raising wages to levels that have given the workforce a degree of independence in their relations with management. Fundamental shifts in the power balance between the workers and their bosses are involved. But, far from taking a leading part, unions are firmly stuck in the traditional role. By insisting that the main area for negotiation between the two sides shall remain the work/wage bargain with a union victory taking the form of an increase along the single dimension of pay, the unions are failing their members — and arguably making themselves redundant.

This process is most evident in Britain, where the unions have enjoyed a high degree of protection from the law. And it appears in the growth of an unofficial structure which is frequently in opposition to the official national structure, and exercises more real power. The Industrial Relations Act of 1971 attempts to curb the growing "lawlessness" among union members by introducing a rule of law into areas previously exempt. It is too soon to guess how successful the law will be, except that as an infringement of immemorial rights it will be bitterly resisted in its application. But the very fact of a parallel unofficial structure draws attention to the inadequacies of the official one.

Unions were formed to secure the power of collective action for workers. Their first priority was to secure some symmetry in bargaining with employers; and the bargaining was mainly confined to the issue of pay, the most urgent concern of the members. That habit still persists, but conditions have changed. Workers in many industries are not struggling to improve starvation wages but to gain increases in wages that are already substantial. This is true of many industries in the USA; and in Britain some of the most strike-prone are the most prosperous: motors and printing. In less secure industries, in Britain's Northeast, for example – the emphasis is less on higher wages than it is on job security and insistence on heavy overmanning.

But the most urgent problems now facing workers in industry derive from the organization of work. The engineering students (of Chapter 4) have chosen to translate their potential surplus earnings as engineers into the perceived advantages of other jobs, or simply keeping their options open during their college career. The unions have failed to make a similar switch of emphasis for their members. The rumbling discontent among assembly line workers indicates that there are improvements to press for other than the incessant demand for increased pay which seems to have little effect even as palliative. More money or better working conditions both represent costs to the company; but conditions represent one-half the waking existence of the workers.

The 1971 strike at the Ford Motor Company in Britain was accompanied by a carefully argued case presented by the Transport and General Workers Union for more money, based on the company's profits and rising costs of living. There was not a word about changing conditions of work that are arguably among the most dehumanizing in industry. The same union argued in the same way with Imperial Chemical Industries. Thus, ironically, the unions are playing the game of the companies in three ways:

- They fight within the rules of the existing work/wage bargain without questioning them.

- They do not fight for changes in the area of work organization that offers the greatest potential rewards for their members.

- By persisting in accepting the priority to maximize monetary reward for work, they tie their members all the more securely to the wheel of the consumption society.

Meanwhile, as we shall see in the next chapter, it is the management that is offering most opportunity for reexamining the rules. In Britain it has been at the insistence of management that Shell, I.C.I., and Philips have all negotiated contracts that go some way beyond anything the unions have demanded. In the USA the most enlightened employers are to be found among those employing nonunion labor; elsewhere, the unionized companies depend on the unions to keep order among their workers (something that would be beyond the powers of the British unions). The point is that the unions are in danger of losing their real purpose — the interest of their members — while still pursuing the traditional aim, rooted in the ancient conflict between workers and employers, that of increasing pay. They bear the institutional marks of any system seeking survival.

The conclusion for the unions could be a grim one. If they fail to represent the real interests of their members, they are offering informal grassroots structures — and management — an opportunity to take the initiative which could seriously threaten their power. An increasingly frustrated workforce will seek outlets in more unruly behavior. In Britain the Donovan Commission recognized that a substantial measure of power had already moved into the hands of the shop stewards; the 1971 Industrial Relations Act is an attempt to force it back into the hands of the national offices, along US lines. But it is questionable whether any such attempt to turn back the clock can succeed. One may speculate that over time the unions could turn into organizations with the single honorific function of agreeing work contracts while the many other issues of their members' work are dealt with through different bodies.

SUMMARY

The characteristic form of change within organizations is enforced: it is a reaction by management to crises which demand solutions. These solutions may change organization practice, and many such changes amount to substantial shifts.

The crises that trigger the changes occur when a changed environment impinges on organization practice through the agency of its members, or as in the Allied Minories case, when changed commercial circumstances force an organization to reappraise traditional practices and assumptions. The changes in the environment relevant to members may take the form of new expectations, although these change slowly; they may be imported by new entrants from different cultures, as from colleges; they may represent the interaction between the possibilities of the nonwork world and the limitations of a job; most commonly and powerfully they can arise from changes in the labor market, presented by the unions as demands for higher pay.

As with other managerial decisions, it is when such crises, presenting him with problems for immediate solution, occur that a manager faces the most urgent pressures. It is a process of change in which unions might be expected to play a leading and initiating role, but it is one in which they are reluctant to engage. In this way, by remaining within the existing assumptions about the wage/work bargain, unions are failing their members.

12
SOCIAL CHANGE AND THE MANAGER: UNION INITIATIVES

If the unions have failed, as I have suggested, it is not for want of trying to press far more radical solutions to the problem of ownership and control than anything proposed in this book. What is ironic is that their very considerable success in raising the pay and living-standards of their members has had to be achieved within the existing framework of relationships and shows few signs of straying outside it. The more direct political solutions proposed by movements within the union structure itself – Guild Socialism, Syndicalism, and now Workers' Control – have been entirely unsuccessful.

I have suggested that the unions, having achieved a partial success, are likely to be trapped within it and that the most far-reaching changes in working patterns, relationships, and job design are more likely to be offered voluntarily by management than they are to be imposed or enforced by militant unions. But this is an incomplete picture. Relevant models of change in which the unions have played an active role range along a continuum stretching from public ownership and worker control in Yugoslavia to "codetermination" in Germany. Since these contain elements which are relevant to modes of change described in the next chapter, they will be briefly examined here.

The Yugoslavian example is an extreme case, interesting mainly because it sets limits to possible models of change. True worker control on the Yugoslavian model is unlikely to be met in the West this side of a revolution. The main feature is that industry in Yugoslavia is "social property" and not, as in other Communist countries, "state property." Thus, while the state has influence exercised largely through the League of Communists, and draws on company profits through taxes, it does not directly control each company. The management runs the company but is appointed and subject to the control of the Workers' Council, probably the most influential body in the factory. Other groups involved are the unions and the Youth Organizations. Jiri Kolaja writes:

> "Yugoslavs maintain that in their system the locus of decision-making has been brought back to the factory and that the distance between managerial decisions and their implementation has been considerably shortened . . . Whereas stockholders are remote from managers in Western corporations, the Yugoslav system has made managers directly responsible to employees who are directly selected from the workplace. . ."*

Since Kolaja's studies more than ten years ago, there has been a considerable shift of emphasis back to a Western-style interest in profit as a measure of efficiency. Managers have been allowed more freedom than in the past to develop, as entrepreneurs, approved industries — particularly tourism — with a minimum of official interference. But, however much the rules may be modified, social ownership and worker control remain important facts of Yugoslav life; it seems unlikely that industry would be allowed to revert to anything resembling capitalist ownership.

Nothing similar to this system is found in the West. A handful of firms are jointly owned by the workers — the John Lewis Partnership in Britain or the Bader Commonwealth, for example. But setting these up has affected ownership only and has been done by particularly idealistic men; they do not contain implications for the organization of work. Political movements working within the unions and political system aim to overthrow capital (among other things). But even though the Workers' Control Movement, for one, is as specific in its aims as the name suggests, I shall not do more than mention them here. They are more concerned with the political issues surrounding the ownership of capital and the disparities

---

*Kolaja, Jiri, *Workers' Councils: the Yugoslav Experience.* London: Tavistock, 1965.

of wealth, and the power that goes with it, than they are with the design of work. Moreover, they have not shown themselves to be strong enough at this stage to pose a threat to the existing system* except where, as in France and Italy, the Communist Party has real strength. The workers' control movement has, however, been involved in some industrial disputes in Britain: some of the problems encountered in the Allied Minories case were attributed by management to the involvement of militant shop stewards in the movement. The seizure of control in 1971 by communist-led shop stewards at the Upper Clyde Shipyards when it was bankrupt and threatened with liquidation provides an isolated example of direct action. But again, these actions have been motivated by the wish to gain possession of jobs where the jobs were threatened by commercially based decisions — that is, to subordinate capital to the workers' need for employment — rather than with nuances about what the jobs comprised.

There have, however, been some moves in Europe toward introducing worker representation into management decisions: the codetermination laws of Germany; worker-directors in the nationalized British Steel Corporation; and a law for Norwegian companies, introduced in October, 1971. Of these the German laws, introduced in 1951 and 1952, and the B.S.C. directors represent the extreme of minimal representation; the Norwegian law, modeled on developments in Norsk Hydro, is closer to the pattern of participation in management that will be the subject of the next chapter.

WORKER-DIRECTORS

There are two main features to the German laws: the requirement that all establishments above a certain size should have Works Councils to which representatives would be elected by company employees; and the requirement that one-third of the members of the Supervisory Board (one-half in the steel and coal industries) should be workers' representatives.

1. The Councils exist to promote harmonious relations between management and employees, mainly through discussion of social and welfare matters. Neither the union powers of negotiation over substantive issues of

---

*This is not to say that conditions of alienation from work and increasing prosperity would not provide fertile ground for radical — even revolutionary — seeds in the absence of some more imaginative initiatives from employers and unions.

pay and conditions nor the management powers in the conduct of the business are affected. The official view is that the Councils have exercised a beneficial influence and helped to maintain peace on the shop floor. But this depends on local conditions. As with many attempts to introduce some worker representation without giving the representative bodies responsibility or power, they more often become talking-shops without real influence.

2. The existence of worker-directors has probably been more influential. On the Supervisory Board* the workers represent the labor interest and provide access to financial and other data for the company. This has substantially improved the level and realism of negotiations between unions and industry.

The British Labor Government introduced something of the sort into the Board structure of British Steel upon nationalization. The four area boards had worker-directors appointed to them. However, the boards were mainly advisory, since the Group Managing Director could not be outvoted. The B.S.C. Chairman, Lord Melchett, explained at the time of their appointment: "The Corporation is hoping that the employee directors will, in an atmosphere of complete confidence and access to all facts, figures, and arguments, bring the Group Board the point of view of the great mass of people working in the industry. . ." However, he went on, the directors were "serving in a personal capacity . . . and not as elected representatives. . ." Such is the paradox at the heart of this way of securing a voice for the worker in the deliberations of management.

A Board of Directors has a quite specific function comprising a range of duties laid down in law and the collective responsibility for decisions that secure the long-term interests of the company. As was pointed out in evidence to the Donovan Commission,† the appointment of workers as directors introduces conceptual conflict over the definition of this function. In Germany it had led to problems of divisions of loyalty in what ought to be collective Board decisions. If, for example, a decision has to be taken over the shutdown of some aging plant, the worker-directors *as*

---

*German companies have a two-tier Board structure. The Supervisory Board (Aufsichtsrat) meets four or five times a year. It appoints the Executive Board (Vorstand), is responsible for the accounts and for major policy decisions. Real power resides with the Executive Board, which has responsibility for the running of the company.

---

†The Royal Commission which reported in 1968 on industrial relations in Britain.

representatives must oppose it since the move will result in a loss of jobs for their constituents; as Board members, however, they may well support the proposal. The evidence concluded that such sectional representation is out of place.

However, there is now pressure from unions in Germany for extending this form of representation up to the levels of the coal and steel industries. This move is being resisted by industrial interests, who see in it an end to German democracy. And it could become of some importance throughout Europe: the German government is insisting that similar provisions be included in the statutes of the "European Company," presently being drafted by the E.E.C. Commission in Brussels. Certainly the appointment of worker-directors has political attractions, providing the appearance of representation even if the reality is necessarily limited by the inherent conflicts.

AUTONOMOUS GROUPS

The crucial drawback of the system of representation discussed above is that it does not realistically deal with the need to give people more of a say in the decisions that affect their lives. It is an improvement, no doubt, to provide a mechanism for expressing popular feeling at Board level. But the appointment of a worker-director spans many intermediate levels of decision-making, each of which more closely affects the voter. Yet he has no influence at these levels, even though through his vote he may formally have some power over them all. It is the same problem that is sapping at the credibility of Western democracy: how can a structure be devised that provides people with a say in the decisions that directly affect them?

Many different "OD-type" approaches have been suggested, and some of them will be discussed in Chapter 13. For the purposes of this chapter, which deals with forces for change that manifest themselves from the bottom up, the law which will shortly, at the time of writing, be debated in the Norwegian Parliament is the most evolved example – indeed the only example in a Western country of "Industrial Democracy." This is a term used to described systems of work, political in origin, which are designed to give more power of self-determination to the worker. It is an important part of the Norwegian picture that the industrial scene is dominated by strong, centrally managed unions with a history since the 1920's of active campaigning to secure representation in management decisions. The result has been a system of highly organized, and for the most part peaceful, negotiating procedures characterized, as in Sweden, by debate between equal parties and arbitrated where necessary by a government with substantial powers.

Although it is not possible at this stage to discuss the Norwegian Bill, its form has been heavily influenced by an experiment at the fertilizer company, Norsk Hydro – part of the nationalized electricity undertaking. By 1966 the company had been through ten years of declining productivity, as a result of which drastic cuts in manpower were proposed by a consultant. Concurrently with the demanning exercise, two plants were selected for an experiment overseen by Professor Thorsrud of the Oslo Work Research Institute. These plants were geographically isolated, recently built, and not directly affected by demanning. Management and the local trade unions appointed a committee of six people with no clear goals except to devise ways of working that would maximize the use of the company's human and technological resources.

The team's approach had a number of familiar features: meticulous information-gathering; frequent meetings with workers and supervisors from the plant under discussion; general meetings; an unceasing effort to make what was being attempted fully understood at all levels and to elicit any worries or objections. In retrospect the management claimed that the two prerequisites of success were commitment from line management and a willingness to take the lead, and the existence of strong and influential union leadership. Workers attached great importance to the frequent meetings, which were vital as a means of generating trust and commitment.

The system that emerged was quite different from anything Norsk Hydro had operated before. Work was organized into autonomous groups within which there was to be a high degree of flexibility. In a sense this pattern came naturally from the nature of the plant: large continuous-process units, relatively sparsely populated by process workers and maintenance teams and grouped around "information centers," typically the control rooms. But what was important was the high degree of self-rule allowed once the decision to set up production groups was made.*

Training. Supervisors were highly trained (200 hours each) in order to relate their job better to the operation of the factory. Workers were given the opportunity to attend training sessions for the same purpose, although

---

*For an overview of this work see Thorsrud, E., "A Strategy for research and social change in industry: A report on the Industrial Democracy Project in Norway," in *Social Science Information*, 9(5), pp. 65-90. Paris: Conseil International des Sciences Sociales.

not during working hours. The training was reinforced by job rotation within the groups, so that members were interchangeable; and between the groups, to provide an understanding of the complete operation. The mechanics of rotation were left for the groups to decide themselves.

Payments. The scale was greatly simplified. Workers were paid according to their abilities (which reflected voluntary training undertaken), to be decided by group supervisor and shop steward. A bonus incentive scheme was introduced on a group basis. The control parameters answered to the requirement: "What does the group influence that is important to the company's objectives?" Suggestions — using measures such as man-hours, output, quality, cost, and losses — were evaluated with the help of the costing department.

Feedback. The information system was arranged so that data on control parameters (also affecting the bonus) was rapidly available at the lowest levels. Telephones were installed at all key points.

Maintenance. A vital function in process plants, the maintenance teams were included with the production groups. Process and maintenance workers acquired each other's skills (to about 60 percent transferability).

The result was a structure composed of highly autonomous groups in which the workers were largely self-supervised. And the supervisors, no longer involved with routine tasks, were free to concentrate on boundary control and regulation: inputs and outputs of the production group. Supervisors are free to allow shifts to operate unsupervised if they are needed for special projects.

The results for the management have been to increase greatly the difficulties of managing, in the sense that it is a more demanding job. "There is no divine right of managers any longer," one manager said, "you have to earn your right to executive authority." The main point of pressure is the morning meetings in which a record of actions to be taken emerges for wide circulation.

The project has been difficult for the company to evaluate, since the experiment overlapped with the productivity and demanning exercise. However, productivity improved; plans were beaten by substantial margins; turnover and absenteeism figures dropped. These last reflected the attitudes of the men, about which there was no question. The most striking change has been in the degree of commitment to the job and the willingness to take responsibility.

The single most crucial feature of this experiment has been the focusing of attention on the work group as the basic unit of the organization, the design of "socio-technical" systems on the Tavistock model. Giving the group autonomy within the limits of the company's objectives has changed the relations of the men to management and the roles of supervisors and shop stewards. It is no millenium, but it represents a solid move toward the peculiarly Scandinavian ideal of industrial democracy.

JOINT CONSULTATION

An attempt is being made in Imperial Chemical Industries in the UK to establish some form of worker representation based in work groups. At a simple structural level, recognizing the central importance of work groups, the new "Joint Consultation" procedures have much in common with the Norsk Hydro experiment. The fundamental difference is that the Norsk Hydro groups have been set up for the purposes of performing and managing a job of work, while the ICI move is intended to set up a political structure within the company. As such it is possible to imagine the two purposes moving together, but there are many difficulties.

Joint consultation is intended to replace the old Works Councils set up early in the company's history to provide a channel of communication between the management and workers. But the provision that Councils should not discuss anything falling into the area of union interest progressively robbed them of power and meaning. It is hoped that by using the existing apparatus of shop steward representation (the shop stewards are elected by the union members), this weakness would be overcome. There are many difficulties in the way of satisfactory introduction of the new scheme. The most intractable arises from the split nature of the union movement. There are no industrial unions; each company negotiates with several. The shop stewards, being representatives within individual unions, frequently have members within several work groups.

The experiment is now in the early stages of its development. It is mentioned here as relevant to the concept of organization structure which is based on the fundamental unit of work groups. It is significant that although neither experiment would have been possible without the active cooperation of unions (which varies across the companies, admittedly), the initiatives for these reforms came from management. Yet both are cases of attempts to push more power down into the workforce.

SUMMARY

Although the greatest part of union pressure is exerted to gain more money for members, there is a strong — but mostly ineffective — political motivation seen in occasional attempts to use the unions for their original purpose, to gain political ends. If the management is not prepared to move ahead of the wage/work bargain, these could become important. Falling short of complete revolution, these moves are toward greater participation by the workers in management decisions.

The most extreme model is that of Yugoslavia, where managers are elected. In Germany and in the nationalized British steel industry the existence of worker-directors suggests political tokenism. A more interesting experiment has been carried out at Norsk Hydro in Norway, where workers were put into "autonomous groups" which were self-governing. In Imperial Chemical Industries in Britain an attempt is being made to set up some form of workers' representative structure based on work groups. It is significant that although neither of these experiments would have been possible without union cooperation, they are both initiatives which originated within management.

13
INTERNAL PRESSURES: ANTICIPATING CHANGE

The paradox of planned organizational change is that the need for it is generated at all levels but the responsibility for initiating it must rest with the managers — who are, no less than other people, the enemies of change and guardians of established practice. However, most change programs have originated within management and have been voluntarily offered, sometimes against considerable resistance, to the people whom ultimately they will benefit most. Even the Norsk Hydro "autonomous groups" experiment, in which the unions played an essential role, originated within the management.

Such a statement needs to be heavily qualified, although it is essentially true. Change programs are voluntary only in the sense that they are intended to anticipate conditions which are expected to lead to far worse problems for the company. They originate among management only in the sense that management is in a position to make the decisions that will bring about change. They benefit the workers, sometimes at the expense of managerial prerogatives, but the new conditions are expected to benefit the company and ensure its profitable survival. In fact, the role of managers as initiators of change is less paradoxical than it may seem, and not just because the role of management has been so defined by such philosophers of business as Peter Drucker. ("Managers of change" is a useful definition but one which does not allow for the innate conservatism of social systems.) For only managers are equipped by training and by their position in the company to take this responsibility:

1. The senior manager has two sorts of *knowledge:*

    • He sees the company as a whole and in the context of its environment.

    • He has a wider range of possible models for change to draw upon, through his more elaborate education and access to expert resources inside and outside the company.

2. The manager has the *power* to make the crucial decisions that set change processes in motion. He can marshal resources and apply them to what he, in agreement with other managers, sees as the benefit of the company.

3. It is the manager's *role* to make the decisions that will secure the company's well-being.

Problems that arise within the workforce do not emerge uncoded, but as symptoms: as union demands, usually for more pay, or as high turnover, absenteeism, and low productivity. The natural response of managers, always working to deadlines, is simply to react to the symptoms as presented — resist the union demands; change the production technology so that a trained chimpanzee could do the jobs. It is a basic law of management that short-term problems drive less obviously urgent issues to the bottom of the pile. And it is a constant battle for managers to step back from the short-term and see their daily diet of small crises in truer perspective. More insidious, managers are no less the prisoners of their needs, preconceptions, and habits of working than the union members; probably they are more so, since they have a greater investment in the existing system and are to a great extent (if unconsciously) committed to its stability. Thus the Allied Minories case describes a situation in which an urgent need for change on a number of fronts was perceived and accepted among senior managers. The resulting process of change, triggered off by changes in the commercial environment but moving down into the most basic issues of workplace relationships, is continuing still. But it is encountering obstacles in the extreme stability of the attitudes of middle and junior management.

The problems faced by Allied Minories were first experienced as a commercial threat: loss of position in traditional markets and worsening financial results. High costs became the focus of attention, and the company found out that it was weakly placed in relation to the competition and peculiarly vulnerable to increases in wages. It was essential to improve productivity, and a number of studies centered on the issue of pay reform and utilization of labor. Up to this point it had been a purely management initiative. The unions were brought in to help solve the problem, and the pay agreements resulted. However, what started as an attempt to reduce costs in the interests of the company's commercial existence became a full-scale change program, initiated from the center. The compliance of managers was assumed, largely for the reasons listed above: their possession of knowledge, power, and their role within the company. Also, the reward system is able to ensure obedience more completely within management than elsewhere in the company.

The main obstacle to the introduction of the agreement was seen quite accurately as the balky and obdurate refusal of the unions to "sell our birthright" and relinquish cherished rights and privileges. The need to get past that obstacle became the main objective of the program. (This fact reflects the peculiar British circumstances in which nationally negotiated agreements cannot be enforced locally.) And the real objective of radically altering the pattern of work and gaining the commitment of workers took second place. Having secured the agreement of unions throughout the company at some considerable cost both in terms of the time and effort expended and of the expense of "buying out" pockets of resistance, the local management relaxed. They had achieved their target and could get back to the business of running their plants.

This was a very human response to the slackening of tension that followed a period of strain. It was also a reversion to the previous set of ruling attitudes, which had remained substantially untouched by the massive agenda of discussions, conferences, and training programs. Nor, given the extent of the change, should anything else have been expected. In a class-ridden country the managers were being asked to put up for auction many of the rights and privileges which were the mark of their position. And it was among the supervisors and junior managers that most resistance was to be found, just as the most stubborn union resistance to change was encountered from those in areas with a long history of privation. There may have been less to trade away in some absolute sense, but it was all they had.

A senior manager in Allied Minories said that the company would have to revise its view of the time needed for a genuine change from an authoritarian mode to a more participative mode. He estimated that it would take from 10 to 15 years to change management attitudes, an estimate borne out by the extraordinary persistence of old commercial habits long after the circumstances that had given rise to them had disappeared.

In this the company is not exceptional. Indeed the most exceptional aspect of the case is the fact that a change program was attempted at all. It requires a heroic effort of objective self-analysis for a management to see its company in true perspective and to accept the need for their own change no less than that of the rest of the company. Earlier in this section I discussed the extraordinary stability of social systems, reinforced by the complexity of the interrelationships within them. How stable they are is demonstrated by the fact that change programs such as Allied Minories are exceptional and not the rule, as one might expect them to be in a time of rapid social change.

In a recent unpublished survey* Alan Wilkinson of Imperial Chemical Industries found 17 companies in Europe actively engaged in experiments in motivation. This did not comprise an exhaustive list, but he points out that the menu of well-known experiments commonly cited in discussion on the subject is more limited still: only the work at three companies in Europe – Philips, Imperial Chemical Industries and A.T.&T. – is at all widely known. A point of subsidiary interest which casts a light on the importance of cultural and other environmental factors is the fact that Wilkinson was unable to find any European experiments in motivation outside the Northern countries: Scandinavia, Holland, and Great Britain. The need for change is more widely recognized in the USA, where new ideas are more easily accepted (another cultural factor) than in Europe. But even so, considering the magnitude of the change in US society, the vast majority of organizations do not accept the fact of change as a constant presence now and in the future.

I have suggested that all major change in the organization is to some degree enforced. The form it takes is determined by voluntary management decisions which are not likely to be made, however, in the absence of some crisis that demands remedial action. Declining productivity or a loss

---

*Wilkinson, A., "A Survey of Some Western European Experiments in Motivation," Institute of Work Study Practitioners, 9/10 River Front, Enfield, Middlesex, England.

of competitiveness in major markets, the occurrence of strikes, high turnover, and absenteeism are some of the conditions which spur management to look at the human side of the organization for ways of cutting costs, seeking peace, or simply finding better methods of doing what has to be done. But the crisis will not carry a program with it: it pinpoints a problem and imposes a penalty for not solving it. The distinction I have made between the forces for change manifesting themselves "bottom-up" or "top-down" is therefore somewhat arbitrary. Forces for change that thrust up from the shop floor are experienced as problems; top-down pressures are experienced as solutions, or at any rate as initiatives. The "autonomous groups" experiment at Norsk Hydro, and other Scandinavian experiments in which the unions have been as much the initiators as management, reflect the special union conditions. The strong centrally run unions — with a long history of negotiation as equals with strong employers' federations — have acquired the role of leading change rather than actively resisting it.

This suggests a role for management and a changed role for the unions. It also suggests a change in some basic assumptions about organizational stability.

ROLE OF MANAGEMENT

If changes in the company's social and political environment carry implications for the organization, it is the job of management to identify these and, if possible, anticipate them. But before a manager can identify the implications for the organization, he must understand the implications for himself and confront the threat this poses to established values and relationships. He must understand what it is in him that resists change; he must understand the nature and dynamics of the group of which he is a part; he must learn to "aim off" for the tendency in himself and others to lag behind change — the slippage between his perceptions of a world as composed of more or less stable systems and the real world of continual change.

Managers must learn a new job, that of scanning their environment for the elements of change that will be significant for the organization. They must scan it for the externally generated pressures that will change the role of the company: the shifts in government policy, the pressures of consumer groups. They must scan it for the signs of new systems which will manifest themselves internally: shifts in the labor market, in value systems, educational patterns. In scanning the environment, they must realize that the new systems will be disguised and that a conscious effort is needed to see them for what they are. And they must set decisions with long term consequences in a context of the future; there is no point in building the most tightly engineered assembly line in the world if in ten years it will not be possible to hire the men to run it.

I am not suggesting a change of heart in the manager, nor advocating a newly moral, still less altruistic, basis for decisions that affect their employees. The reward system within which managers operate is likely to remain unchanged in all important respects for many years yet. The market will continue to reward efficient operation, the shareholders to applaud profits. But the changes I have touched upon will appear as constraints on an organization's freedom of action and eventually on its capacity to survive.

It is not enough simply to make the intellectual effort of perceiving a need for change and then making a decision that other people should change. (Pollution is something *other* people do, it is the *other* drivers who are dangerous. "What, me?" senior managers say; "*My* attitudes don't need changing!") Without the commitment of the top managers there will be no change in the organization culture, and change elsewhere will be slow and uncertain — as has been demonstrated by follow-up studies on the permanence of attitude changes in T-Groups, which can show a partial reversion on return to an unchanged environment. Without a positive attitude at the top of the company there is little hope that the junior — and more threatened — managers will do more than pay lip service. And junior managers and foremen comprise the interface with the workers, whose attitudes and commitment to the organization are the ultimate focus of attention in a change program. There are more of them, they are the producers in the company, and theirs is the domain where the need for internal change is most strongly felt.

There is an alternative for managers, the alternative chosen by the oil companies in the Middle East and described in Case 2. The forces for change are perceived and perhaps accurately seen to lead to a complete disruption of the existing system; the strategy chosen is not adaptation to the new circumstances but resistance and delay. While in a pragmatic sense this may be an intelligent strategy for oil companies operating in foreign countries — strategy based in a clear-eyed view of an inevitable loss of power and profit — it is not so realistic for a company that hopes to remain in long-term existence in its home base. Yet it is implicitly the strategy adopted by the many companies whose policy is to deal with the symptoms of change — strikes, high turnover, low productivity — rather than confront the causes — alienation from the work and a more discriminating and demanding workforce. The first leads to tighter integration, stricter controls, and the design of jobs in which skill becomes minimally important; the counterpart of this is close attention to Herzberg's "hygiene" factors. Companies adopting this strategy (which means at this moment most companies) will find themselves weak bidders in an increasingly discriminating labor market, for the processes of change in society will steadily continue to shift the balance against work that subordinates people to machines and allows them no say in deciding how they shall achieve their tasks.

In many, probably most, industries the process will be long and pragmatism will rule; that is, the company will yield reluctantly to the pressures for change, usually too late to gain any benefit from the act of concession. (In Allied Minories one of the strongest arguments accepted by the Board for changing was the certainty that change would come anyway; the company could gain from leading, rather than lagging.) Where the production process is highly systems-engineered, as it is in the motor industry, a change of practice will seem not only radically disruptive but also impossibly expensive. And so long as there exists a workforce which will remain within the traditional work/wage framework, the companies are likely to remain within the well-understood framework of steadily mounting trouble, periodical crises, and buying off the workers' alienation. The obstacles to change seem huge, and there is little inducement to make changes if costs are increased. Managers get no rewards for bankrupting a company, however humane the cause.

But the responsibility of watching for the company's long-term interests remains. And it may be necessary to accept short-term increases in cost in the interests of some more distant benefit. Indeed, the pattern of high initial costs is characteristic of radical change programs. And where there are special factors, the cost can be higher still. In Allied Minories, for example, the pay agreement was designed to meet the needs of the company's most skilled workers, crucial to its future. But within the company there were a number of repetitive manual jobs which were quite adequately rewarded within the old payments system. The cost of including these in the new scheme was considerable, but was thought to be unavoidable in the interests of consistency throughout the company. (In fact, some managers now suggest there were other ways through this problem; for example, adopting a more piecemeal approach.) And the effects on product groups in which the technology was such that repetitive manual work predominated has been to raise doubts about their future. However, these were enclaves of untypical practice within a much larger whole. In industries where such jobs predominate, the management may decide not to attempt a massive change, but only while there exists a sufficiently large pool of low-grade unskilled workers with demands no more complex than the opportunity to maximize their earnings.

In the sufficiently long term it is my view that management has no alternative except to reorder the pattern of work to provide the opportunity to achieve more in personal terms than today's industry is accustomed to offering. And the managers ought to lead the change, for the workers will demand what altruism does not provide. Change will eventually be enforced. And there are advantages to meeting the inevitable more than halfway.

SUMMARY

Change programs can originate only within the management. Managers have the knowledge and resources, and it is their role to secure the long-term interests of the company. But this demands a rare capacity for self-questioning, for the managers are themselves the subject for change no less than the rest of the workforce. As a result, the effort does not correspond to the need for change.

The manager must redefine his role in order to perceive the need or change in his environment more consciously; he must learn to watch for the signs that point to emergent systems that could become forces for change; he must learn to anticipate the direction of this change. In the short term, this is only possible for a few companies in special industries or in peculiarly demanding environments. Most industries will be unwilling or unable to make radical changes in patterns of working. But in the end the change will be enforced through the demands of the workforce. And there are advantages in meeting the inevitable more than halfway.

14
DEMOCRATIC ORGANIZATIONS

Companies are entering a period of transition which will be peculiarly taxing for their managers. It is a transition between contracts, legal or informal, which are based in economic coercion and contracts which embody the values of the emerging voluntary society. The transition reflects a shift in the balance of power between institutions and individuals.

It is taxing for managers above all because it so directly threatens the values and assumptions which they have acquired on their way to the top. Yet it is the job of the manager to discern, through the fog of these assumptions, which changes in the environment have energy for change inside the organization, and then to respond realistically to them. At the same time he must avoid the trap of giving change itself a value: changes are only valuable if they contribute to the organization's long-term health.

Deadeningly banal? Consider the following cases of change, how they have been perceived and reacted to, and the threats they carry for the organization.

1. Jim Bleckinshaw III was — still is — a highly ambitious man and more than usually able. His company, one of the world's biggest, had its eye on his career and put him in charge of the important London office at an

early stage. He was outstandingly successful, as he had always been. Over a period of six years, he transformed the British subsidiary and increased profits more than ten times. When he had thus proved himself, he was summoned back to New York, offered a senior job with a place on the Board, and was as good as told that the next stop would be the presidency of the company in four years or so.

Bleckinshaw was dazzled, immensely gratified, yet to his own intense surprise he found himself cast into a state of gloomy confusion. He worried away at this for the next month, during which he hardly slept, and began to see the shape of his doubts under the murk of his unexamined assumptions about job, career, fame, and money. The problem was simplicity itself: he lived well, in a pleasant house outside London; he organized his work to see a lot of his wife and young children; he enjoyed his work, and he liked London. To move to New York meant changing house, changing schools; worse, it meant hours of commuting and travel all over the country; it meant weekend work and less time for the things he was only just learning to enjoy. Worse still, things could only degenerate further. If he got the top job, he would be one of the most highly paid and powerful executives in the world, but virtually without a family and without a home.

Even when he saw these things, Bleckinshaw couldn't accept the logic of his conclusions. The grip of the old ways of thought was too strong. It wasn't until he realized that he was not even going to enjoy the new job that he turned the offer down, resigned, and took a job with a much smaller British competitor. The president of the company was outraged: "Jim, you're being irrational," he said at the end of a pretty tight-lipped discussion. "Yes," Jim replied with a sense of relief, "I'm being completely emotional."

Well may the company president have been tight-lipped. From his end, Bleckinshaw's action was mad and dangerous. It was mad because, instead of leaping with glad cries at a brilliant opportunity, he was choosing to vegetate in a small offshore island near Europe; and dangerous because it was so opposed to the company's norms and potentially threatening to its structure. If the best people are not motivated to struggle up the ladder by what they will get when they reach the top, companies could find themselves short of best people. A very imperfect selection takes place, as it has in politics on both sides of the Atlantic. For the process of politics is so deeply distasteful to many people that, regardless of the real importance of the job to be done, the top ranks tend to be filled by those whose main qualification is their willingness to persist through it.

The conclusions are twofold. First, and at the simplest level, such decisions are becoming more widespread and the old assumptions about managerial motivation may not last for long. Second, if these changes are (as I believe them to be) a result of greater financial security and concurrent shifts in values, it is the companies who are going to have to make an adjustment. The main adjustment lies in balance between expectations — the company's and the manager's. Total devotion to work and sharp-toothed ambition were once the minimum basic equipment of a young man wanting to get on, not just because they were useful qualities but also for their value as recognition signals. This is still largely true, but companies should give some thought to the mix of satisfactions which even their most highly motivated men will be wanting from their lives.

Bleckinshaw knew that if he did get to the top spot, he would be better off financially but worse off in many other areas. There is a limit to the number of Cadillacs a man can drive at one time, to paraphrase a Moldavian proverb, and little pleasure to be gained from keeping spare ones in the garage. Moreover, when the job means constant travel and living in hotels — albeit first-class travel and luxury hotels — there may be only retirement to look forward to. Two questions thus arise: Are these sacrifices cost-effective for the individual? And are they necessary for the good management of the company? Many of them have no basis in real needs but are manifestations of a work ethic that is now relaxing its grip. Perhaps the executives should work four-day weeks, or work from home; perhaps a different structure of the corporation can be designed which would create different demands on executives' time and allow for smaller units in which work and non-work life are more integrated; perhaps companies should learn to accept, and not condemn, the executives who peel off to sit on some rung halfway up the ladder, and be glad that they are around to do the work they want to do.

This is the nub: in a voluntary society, it is increasingly the executive who will do the choosing.

2. Sharper pressures are being generated in the organization by the demands of new recruits. Their expectations are and always have been unrealistically high. But whereas it was once assumed that the new recruit, exposed to the socializing influences of work in the organization, would learn different ways, it is now the company who is learning to adjust.

Instead of regarding the new entrant as an unripe executive who needs only to be left on the shelf in a warm dark place to become usable, they are being forced by these demands — and by the sometimes frightening mobility of new hires — to provide different, more flexible, autonomous work.

The change has been coming for a long time, although it is only relatively recently that the campus attitudes have begun to bite. A fairly typical story is that of Dick Cottier who, like many new graduates, joined a large company more because its size, the range of possible activities, and a training scheme seemed to leave options open than for the prospects it offered. Reality was less flexible. He was in a department which had been newly formed on the recommendation of some text-bound consultant, but for which there was neither real work nor appropriate staff for the theoretical function. Morale was very poor and Cottier left, as many had left before him.

He was sympathetically "debriefed" by two of his bosses, one of whom he'd not met before, and then taken for the ritual terminal chat to the Personnel Manager, a distinguished-looking man with a good war record. The Personnel Manager listened gravely, shook his head sadly at appropriate moments, and pronounced himself shocked at the story which only confirmed what other ex-employees had told him on their way out of the door. Cottier then went to see the Personnel Director, less easily shockable but seemingly ignorant of the circumstances that were resulting in a 45 percent annual turnover of graduate trainees.

The Director briefly left the office at one point, considerately giving Cottier the chance to read the memo on his desk. It was from the old soldier and started: "I have spoken to A----- and S---- about Cottier's departure. They are agreed that he is no loss to the company. . . " And it went on to explain that Cottier was a "congenital malcontent." All of this may have been true, but there was not a word about the earlier conversation; there was no information about the seething discontent downstairs, only the soothing noises appropriate to a senior manager's ear.

The company has since substantially changed its policy toward new hires. The Personnel Manager and Director both retired early. Their successors made a start by greatly reducing the number of graduates taken on, from a formless annual influx of "graduate material" to levels more closely geared to the company's needs and job opportunities. The pattern of early employment has been changed from an initial five years' osmotic acculturation to involvement in something like a real job. The change is by no means complete, but it already represents a radical departure from the pattern of only five years ago. And it demonstrates how the insistent demands of recruits – once completely without power or status – were able to force quite important changes.

The immediate response of the managers also demonstrates how organizations move to oppose changes to existing relationships. The way information is filtered as it passes up and down through an organization has often been commented on. The way in which it is *excluded*, simply by not being recognized for what it is, is less obvious. A group of disaffected recruits will appear to the eyes of experience as little more than a nuisance. The instinctive response is to take action to restore the status quo: crudely, by applying the pressures of discipline (withholding pay increases, putting in bad reports); more gently, by buying the problem out (promotion, conferring meaningless titles) or simply by letting the disaffected employees go.

None of these courses of action requires deeper probing of the system, which remains fundamentally untouched. The problem of why trainees, once so grateful and hardworking, had become demanding and difficult had to wait for analysis until the company was forced by a crisis to look at it. But by that time, when all attempts to restore the status quo had failed, the company had gone through a costly experience. This is a case where a realistic view of changes in the company environment would have set up warning signals, and where changes in company ahead of the crisis would have been justified.

3. It is one thing to change systems to accommodate the demands of the small and important group of newly hired graduates. It is quite another to change whole manufacturing systems in response to similar demands from the mass of the workforce. But this is the prospect being faced by such industries as motors, where the problems created by the assembly line are receiving growing recognition; but solutions are sparse.

With the active support of their unions, the companies are propping up the status quo. Discipline having lost most of its meaning as a control device in conditions of full employment (or the expectation of full employment, which amounts to the same thing in terms of behavior), motor companies are buying out the disaffection of their workers and devising ways to neutralize the effects of their high labor turnover. Yet it is hard to see how the existing arrangements of assembly lines can continue in the developed Western countries. In spite of high wages, the workforce comes from the most economically disadvantaged part of the populations: in Detroit from the blacks, and in Germany and Sweden –

the two European countries with the highest standards of living – from immigrants. The gap between the expectations of an affluent, well-educated population and the reality of working life offered by much of modern industry is bound to give rise to the troubles we are experiencing. But major changes will be made only when a crisis point has been reached which will generate energy enough to overcome the internal resistances of the organization. In the motor industry it will be a financial crisis: the cost of labor, strikes, and a high reject rate will rise to a point where alternative systems will look attractive.

It is tempting to assume, as some commentators do, that the change must be inevitably in one direction – toward enriching the workers' jobs – or that because it seems morally right to do that, the companies should not wait for their energizing crisis. However, this view limits the range of possibilities open to the companies; it ignores the fact that the most enriched jobs in the world are of no use in a bankrupt company; and, by stressing the importance of enriching *work*, it leaves out the possibility of seeking other ways to enrich the workers' *lives*.

Evidence is accumulating that the somewhat utopian assumption that everybody has a latent wish to seek self-actualization in their work may not be realistic. Many would as soon take the opportunities offered by shorter working hours and higher pay to self-actualize away from the job, putting up with routine and meaningless work as the price they pay. This may be just as well: not all work is capable of being enriched without imposing unacceptable costs elsewhere in the system. And it opens up a different route of development for industries like motors.

It could be that the experiments at Volvo and Saab in Sweden will allow what they promise – the development of radically different techniques for car assembly. But it could also be that the cost of turning the assembly line over to teams that build whole cars, or regrouping tasks along the line to provide greater variety in the work is acceptable only for building relatively low-volume, high-cost, specialized cars – like Volvo and Saab. The companies which produce for the mass market, where fractions of cents count, have still the option of continuing down the road of engineering optimization and of continuing to buy off the workers with more money and then the four-day week, until labor costs have risen to a point where it pays to automate completely.

This is a rather harder-faced view of the direction of industrial change, since it assumes that companies will, and should, only make changes that are consistent with their own long-term health. In a voluntary society changes made only on quasi-moral grounds may be undesirable, if threatening to the company; they are also unnecessary, since the worker has the freedom to pursue his own self-interest without the intervention of others.

4. A different sort of adjustment is needed between the company and its environment. In the case of the oil companies in the Middle East, I suggested that the companies based their policies on the view that they had no place there in the long term; I also pointed out that this doubtless accurate assessment was based on the assumption that they could not change their basic form or status. Had they been prepared to offer changes, it is possible – no more than that – that they would be more strongly placed. Alternatively, it has been suggested that to withdraw altogether would have placed them still more strongly. It is enjoyable to speculate. It would have been more useful if such speculation had come before the event.

This is something an increasing number of companies, watching with dismay the accelerating rate of change, are now prepared to do. A fairly typical example might be one giant multinational company which has recently started looking at likely developments in its commercial and political environment 10 to 15 years ahead. Drawing up a series of possible futures around probabilistic forecasts for the variables that most interest them, the planners have been able to make guesses about the most satisfactory form and position that the company should assume. This in turn suggests actions that need to be taken now in order to get them moving in the desired direction.

The exercise has yielded some startling results. The forecasters have been able to point ahead to the near-certainty of radical changes in the company's political environment, in particular its relationship with governments. This in turn has suggested that the company's great size – a source of pride and of considerable strength – may become a positive disadvantage and that the company should consider adopting a conscious policy of "hiving-off" operating companies into separate subsidiaries with local shareholders – reducing its real size. The policy of vertical integration, also a historic source of strength, has been vigorously challenged.

Another large company in a related field has carried out a similar exercise, working within a shorter time span, and has also emerged with the conclusion that it should split into smaller units, although for quite different reasons. In this case the argument is not political but practical: it has grown too large to be managed effectively; moreover, the sorts of local pressures developing and union demands for a higher degree of local autonomy make some separation attractive. Yet it too had drawn considerable strength in the past from its sheer bulk.

Both of these companies have become aware of the importance to them of their environment. Both have reached conclusions that represent radical departures from accepted values and point to major changes in company policy. Other companies may not face such discontinuous changes but all are facing a future in which the external environment, increasingly turbulent, is crowding up to their windows.

In Chapters 8 and 9, we discussed some of these influences: pollution, conservation, consumerism, and so on. Such issues represent demands, or groups of demands, from the organization's "stakeholders" — those groups which have points of contact and interchanges with the organization. Until recently it was possible to assume that those interchanges were adequately ruled and controlled by competition in the markets: the labor market, the market for the company's products, the market for land downstream or downwind of a polluting plant, the market for investment. All of these transactions were assumed to be self-regulating. It is a measure of the turbulence of the company environment that this is no longer true: the full and complex demands of the environment cannot be assumed away any more.

This can best be seen in terms of the company's objectives. These have been set traditionally in terms of financial returns. It is a powerful simplification and has been adequate for many purposes. But it only allows explicit consideration of the needs of one group of stakeholders, the shareholders. As the insistent demands of the others mount, they will have to be included in the company objective structure. The company mentioned at the beginning of this section has found itself, looking ahead, having to lay great stress on the developments in the political environment — so much so that they could determine the shape of the company. Developments in the motor industry will be increasingly dominated by factors arising from the needs of the workforce. Heavy polluters, like paper mills, where the cost of dealing with the pollution is significant in relation to total costs, will find themselves significantly influenced by the need to satisfy the pollution/conservation lobby. All of these can be seen in the development of more complex structures of objectives which allow the demands and needs of stakeholders their force in company decisions.

All of these are challenges to the companies' adaptive capacity. If the companies cannot meet the demands of their employees or those of the environment internally, they will cease to satisfy these groups and this could threaten their existence. In terms of the managers' own response, the challenge of a changing organizational environment is a challenge to their capacity to learn. The main problem that the manager faces is that of recognizing the unfamiliar for what it is, resisting the natural urge to force it into the mold of his preconceptions. It is a hard thing to ask, since we all live by our experience and cannot simply put it aside. Yet experience has taught that young people with long hair are effeminate and unemployable — which has had to be reinterpreted in terms of company and employee expectations of each other; and these expectations are having to be renegotiated. Experience teaches that workers who strike are irresponsible wreckers who have to be brought back into line with blows or, if these fail, bribes; but companies are having to deal increasingly with the reasons why they strike. Experience teaches that people who complain about pollution are interfering with the free working of the market, that worries about the conservation of natural resources come from little old ladies in tennis shoes, that a man who doesn't want to kick and gouge his way to the top is not worth respect; but none of these (rather exaggerated) stereotypes is going to help us see clearly or to respond realistically to the unfamiliar.

This is the point where I started the book. The future is hidden in our midst, but we have difficulty seeing it because we respond to the new always in terms of our experience. This mechanism — which results in an instinctive resistance to change — has been a vital factor in maintaining the stability of organizations in times when "natural" processes of change were adequate to deal with changes in the environment. But such processes are not adequate to deal with rapid and turbulent change, particularly those changes I have called "non-extrapolative." Stability has meant maintenance of the status quo; now it will have to mean the maintenance of the organization's functioning and that this functioning will include processes of planned change. The organization must build into its working the capacity to redesign itself.

This is not meant to suggest that change is itself a good thing, nor that organizations should (or could) cease to work towards internal stability. Extrapolative change, which follows in more-or-less lawful ways from the observed functioning of existing systems, will continue to dominate our lives. In particular, the processes of "integrative" change, of profit- and efficiency-seeking change, will continue. Companies will continue to grow and to become more international. Government and industry will continue to draw together. Advances in communication technology will allow companies to develop more integrated systems. It is within this framework of forces for change that room will have to be found for the individual — or rather, that room must be created for the individual by his own powers of choice.

The manager, agent of change, organization development consultant, and company planner all stand where these diverse forces for change cross. And it is their job to find the balance between them. The OD expert helps to find the point of balance between the individual and organization; the planner, between the organization and its environment. Each exists to help the company learn.

The final irony in this is that commercial organizations are showing themselves to be more responsive to the changing demands of their members and of society than are the institutions whose job it is to represent them. The development of more democratic modes of operation, devising ways of giving workers a say in those parts of the work which most directly affect them, could be a model for government. The changes have not been voluntarily offered; they have been conceded when mounting pressures have threatened real damage to the organizations. And this is precisely why governments (and unions) have not responded: their survival has not been seriously threatened. Governments are massively stable collections of huge departments, any of which are virtually indestructible. But before pressures mount to crisis point — which has been threatening sporadically throughout the past decade — they could do worse than take a leaf out of the companies' book and learn ways to anticipate change.

OVERVIEW

1. ORGANIZATIONS: STRUCTURE AND BEHAVIOR

Organizations are open systems, existing within their environment through interchange of matter, energy, and information. They are composed of subsystems and are themselves parts of other systems, the systems and subsystems interreacting in complex ways.

Feedback within the systems makes them extremely stable. Constraining forces on a system or attempts to disrupt existing patterns of relationships within it will elicit a response that tends to oppose the direction of change. As a result all systems tend to move toward a condition of internal stability. Which is to say that inasmuch as an organization has an inherent purpose, that purpose is survival. Goals more usually attributed to organizations — growth, profit, return on capital, or the maintenance of the chairman's style of living — are subordinate to this main purpose. They reflect salient uncertainties in the environment, constraints, or the unrestrained fantasies of managers.

This structure means that organizations are inherently insensitive to policy changes within wide limits — the more complex they are, the more insensitive. The natural tendency in managers to respond to problems in ways that deal with the symptoms while leaving untouched the underlying causes shows up in a sharp division between actions appropriate to achieve long- and short-term ends. There is a wide disparity between the long- and short-term consequences of changes in policy and a fundamental incompatibility between the long- and short-term objectives of the organization.

Organizations would be impossible to manage if it was not possible to make simplifying assumptions about many of these complexities. Of these the most important is that managers can make decisions on a closed system basis: the assumption that a decision taken within a particular system (department, factory, company, product group, market) will not affect nor be affected by what is happening outside it — beyond certain obvious connections of an input-output kind. Such partial equilibrium solutions depend on the existence of a stable environment and of "slack" between systems, which allows a degree of relative movement.

The characteristic mode of change in Western industrialized countries has been integrative, and the key characteristic is loss of slack. Partial equilibrium solutions are becoming less satisfactory, particularly where interaction between organizations and their social environment is involved. Consequently, the environment is becoming more of a factor inside organizations and requires more explicit attention.

2. CHANGES IN THE SOCIAL ENVIRONMENT

To anticipate the effects of change, we need to predict its directions. If we knew where to look, we would find the future in our midst. Most of it we can recognize and, on the assumption that these systems will continue to behave much as they have in the past, we can predict how they will be in the future by extrapolation. All mathematical methods of prediction are based on this principle. These systems are enormously predominant and provide the continuity of society, the institutions, ideas, technologies, and relationships whose continued existence in some form can be assumed.

But growing up among them are new or emergent systems whose existence, still less their potential importance, is more difficult to recognize. We cannot see them because at an early stage of development they reveal little of themselves, and what they do reveal is disguised by a habit of growth within existing systems. Moreover, we are certain to misinterpret what we do see: our perceptions are formed by experience, and for this purpose the past is always out of date. Are children delinquent or the harbingers of a new order? Are strikers irresponsible wreckers or an ultimately benevolent force for change inside the organization?

The increasing rate of change in society has brought these problems to the fore, since it has revealed the inadequacy in times of rapid change of the unconscious method by which change was naturally assimilated: responding to what is new when it can no longer be ignored. However, while change is more rapid than in the past, it is still continuous. But the changes in our perceptions – or rather in the models against which we judge reality – are discontinuous. The new systems break through the surface of our perceptions in ways that appear to be discontinuous, although they have been gathering strength in our midst all the time.

The continuity of change stretches back into times that were incomparably different from today's conditions. Since the turn of the century we have been through a period of industrial development during which the landscape of society has changed beyond recognition. Social attitudes and assumptions about what constitutes permissible limits of freedom have been democratized; workers are enjoying privileges previously reserved for the wealthy few; the absolute right of a man to dispose of his property as he wished has been replaced by a view of property that sees it at best as a form of privileged access to resources, contingent on social will; the government has grown enormously in power and complexity, as has the corporation itself; the power of labor has grown in relation to capital.

The question is, what are the forces which have brought about these changes? And how, and in what directions, will they change society in the future? It is tempting but misleading to see change in terms of the issues around which it coalesces: poverty, racism, Vietnam, and the rest. Issues are the seed crystals of change and without power to effect it unless the forces for change are already present, as in a supersaturated solution. Social change is the manifestation of shifts in the underlying systems of values, power, and money in society. Many interdependent influences are active: education, rapid communication and transport, the decline of religion and of the family, increased levels of material aspiration.

These represent systems, some of them with erstwhile power to coerce desired forms of behavior from people through the granting and withholding of rewards. The grip of these systems is slackening with the result that the direction of change is toward more personal freedom. More than anything, the systems are losing their power to coerce because the rising tide of ambient wealth is loosening the grip of the consolidating economic systems. Sanctions available within the economic system have less force in times of prosperity and high employment. And as the secure expectation of material well-being is implanted, they lose even the residual power of old habit. (Temporarily this is strong: men are still moved by their fathers' stories of the Depression.)

People are still driven by and held within the system by the need to satisfy appetites that are to some extent artificially fostered. But their children, having been brought up amidst surplus wealth, are less driven. Students are demanding freedom because they are to a large extent free. But the demands of workers, made within a more restricted range of possibilities, constitute a far more revolutionary force for change within organizations. They may provide a model for social change too.

Although technology and economic forces continue to bind people and systems together in closer interdependencies, the movement toward individual freedom is gaining greater force. We are moving toward a "voluntary" society, in which the involvement with and commitment to the systems of which people are members is a matter of individual choice. It is a change with serious implications for companies since it attacks many of the assumptions on which organizations have been based.

3. PRESSURES ON THE CORPORATION

The pressure of change on the organization today manifests itself internally and externally. External pressures are the most intense and visible and receive the most immediate response from management. These are rising from a generalized mood of disenchantment with the aims of the corporation and the capacity of the market to allocate resources for the provision of such social goods as safe, clean cars; they are rising too from the effects on society and the environment of the continuing growth of population and the rate of consumption. They will manifest themselves as increasingly direct action, possibly leading to limitations on the companies' freedom of action and a redefinition of the role of the corporation in society.

A more organized external pressure on the corporation will come from the continuing process of integration between government and industry in the interests of economic management. Two other areas will be appropriated by the government: Where popular protest has shown the market system to be inadequate for its social purpose — as in the design of cars, already mentioned — the government will act to introduce safeguards for society. The functioning of the regulatory agencies — which have, but often do not perform, the job of safeguarding the interests of society against such specific threats as statutory monopoly — will be tightened. The second area is that of resource management. As land becomes scarcer, the US government must take what European governments already have: more control over the uses to which it is put, setting it in the context of an overall plan. Similarly, controls on companies' and cities' capacity to pollute a diminishing environment are already being introduced.

Forces for change that manifest themselves internally can be further divided into change enforced by demands from employees or voluntarily conceded by management. The distinction is not rigorous, since the forces for change do not manifest themselves with a structured program of action. They tend to emerge as inchoate problems, such as declining competitiveness and disaffection among the workers, in response to which the management "voluntarily" sets a process of change in motion. That the unions, which represent the men, have not been more positive and imaginative in pressing on the management the real needs of their members is a measure of their failure and possibly of their potential redundancy.

This is not a valid generalization at the political level. Unions have always been political bodies and in Europe, though less in the USA, are pursuing such specifically political ends as "Workers' Control." But these movements have something of a period flavor. The active role of unions in Scandinavia, with a long history of taking a leading and responsible role in central negotiations with employers' federations, is more to the point of this book. In these countries the unions have played a leading part in the introduction of experimental systems of working.

The responsibility for leading change processes in the organization must belong to management. It is management that must scan the environment for significant changes; managers, particularly top managers, must be sensitive to the manifestations of changed conditions inside the organization; managers must understand what these conditions mean and where they lead. There is no point in calling striking or inefficient workers "irresponsible" when the return of a "sense of responsibility" can only come from a return of environmental conditions of privation and an acceptance of authority neither possible nor desirable. This is a trebly onerous responsibility for managers. Not only must they initiate and lead change but also, if they are to recognize the need for it, they must first discard habits of thought so deeply ingrained as to be unconscious.

One thing is clear: people will demand more from their lives than they are presently getting. They will demand it because their needs are being expanded through education (of many sorts) and because they have the power to enforce their demands. We are leaving a time when it has been possible to design work for engineering and economic optimality, and only afterwards go to the labor market for the human units to plug into the machine. And it may soon be that the assembly line, that miracle of production engineering, will come to be seen as something from a twentieth-century torture chamber. The troubles that General Motors is having at its Lordstown, Ohio, works — where the highly paid workers have been maliciously damaging the cars they assemble — could be, while deplorable, nonetheless inevitable.

Companies will have the choice of two quite opposed courses for dealing with these changes if they are not to be damaged by them. They can redesign jobs to give workers more satisfaction in their work or they can continue to design the complexity out of the work, offering the workers high salaries and short hours instead of job satisfaction. The choice of course will probably depend on the industry; the motor industry, for example, can go either way — to fully automated assembly lines or to what is being tried in the small Swedish motor company, Saab, the formation of assembly groups. (This is a method of working in which a group of men is responsible for the complete assembly of a car and its testing.) The choice will also depend on the worker. Work may simply become less important in people's scales of values, and they might welcome routine and meaningless work for a relatively small part of their week to be released for self-actualization off the job.

Some of these changes may result in higher production costs, although not necessarily. But if so, the costs will be borne not for reasons of abstract morality but because in a rich society — a voluntary society — offering a wide range of choices people will demand no less.

good ending